Simplicity's

QUICK & EASY SEWING FOR THE HOME

WINDOWS

Simplicity's
QUICK & EASY SEWING FOR THE HOME
WINDOWS

EDITED BY ANNE MARIE SOTO

AND THE

STAFF OF THE SIMPLICITY PATTERN COMPANY

Rodale Press, Inc.
Emmaus, Pennsylvania

OUR MISSION

We publish books that empower people's lives.

RODALE BOOKS

SIMPLICITY

Editor: Anne Marie Soto
Cover and Interior Designer: Christine Swirnoff
Art Direction and Production: Ripinsky & Company
Administrative Manager: Cheryl Dick
Senior Illustrator: Phoebe Gaughan
Illustrator: Deborah Sottile
Copy Editor: Didi Charney
Senior Vice President, Product, Simplicity Patterns: Judy Raymond

RODALE BOOKS

Editor: Susan Weaver
Designer: Patricia Field
Copy Editor: Carolyn Mandarano
Production Coordinator: Jodi Schaffer
Senior Editor, Craft Books: Cheryl Winters-Tetreau
Executive Editor, Home and Garden: Margaret Lydic Balitas
Editor-in-Chief: William Gottlieb

On the cover: Super Simple Swag, page 36
Projects on pages 117–124 designed by Shirley Botsford

If you have any questions or comments concerning this book, please write to:

Rodale Press, Inc.
Book Readers' Service
33 East Minor Street
Emmaus, PA 18098

Library of Congress Cataloging-in-Publication Data

Simplicity's quick & easy sewing for the home. Windows / edited by Anne Marie Soto
and the staff of the Simplicity Pattern Company.
p.   cm.
ISBN 0-87596-676-4 hardcover
1. Drapery. 2. Window shades. 3. Valances (Windows). I. Soto, Anne Marie. II. Simplicity Pattern Co.
TT390.S49 1995
646.2' 1—dc20   94–44847 CIP

Distributed in the book trade by St. Martin's Press

2 4 6 8 10 9 7 5 3 1 hardcover

CONTENTS

INTRODUCTION

Windows! Everybody has them, and everybody wonders what to do with them. Here, within the pages of this book, are 30 beautiful solutions.

We at Simplicity have watched with delight as sewing for the home has become increasingly popular . . . and we've kept a careful eye on the trends that attract the attention of today's decor-savvy consumers. We know that all sewers, regardless of their level of expertise, crave window treatments that offer optimum impact in minimum time. *Quick, easy,* and *fashionable* are the operative words—words we kept in mind when developing the projects for this book.

Most of the curtains and valances in this book have enough built-in fullness to accommodate a range of window widths; many of the drapes puddle slightly on the floor. This means that precise window measurements are not critical elements for successful results. It also means we have been able to eliminate the complicated yardage calculations that most consumers find intimidating. And where window measurements are required or yardage formulas are necessary, we've reduced them to clear, simple steps that anyone can follow.

Each project is introduced with a full-page, four-color photograph and is followed by complete, self-contained instructions, including window dimensions, a supply list with fabric suggestions and yardage requirements, cutting directions, sewing directions, and installation information. For some of these projects, the sewing is optional. The "No-Sew Knotted Swag," "No-Sew Butterfly Swag," and "Super Simple Swag" can all be made entirely at the ironing board, using paper-backed fusible web and our no-sew hemming technique.

"Sew Simple" tips, scattered throughout the book, contain information on tools and techniques for achieving professional results with minimal effort. Some of these tips focus on a specific window treatment; others can be applied to many of the treatments in this book.

And just in case 30 fabulous ideas aren't enough, check out the "Design Plus" tips that are included with the projects. Here's where you discover ways to enhance the design potential of your window treatment by simply changing the fabric, the trim details, the proportions, or the hardware. Professional installation tips are also an important part of this tip series.

"Terms & Techniques" at the back of the book contains additional helpful information. The opening section focuses on the hardware, both practical and decorative, that is used to create our window treatments. If your chosen project calls for some unfamiliar hardware, here's where to look. The balance of this section is devoted to stitching terms, information on cutting bias strips and making bias tape, general stenciling directions, and tying a bow. To take the guesswork out of where this information applies, when your selected window treatment utilizes any of these techniques, the project's instructions will refer you to the appropriate page.

With the projects in this book, it doesn't matter if you are venturing into the world of home dec sewing for the first time or the fiftieth. We've eliminated the guesswork and the tedium and have left you with the fun and excitement of creating beautiful window treatments that will make your home the envy of all who cross its threshold.

Simplicity Pattern Company

VALANCES

There's no need to search high and low for the perfect color-matched fabric when you can stencil your own beautiful coordinating border.

BOW BEAUTIFUL

Window Size:

24" to 40" (61cm to 102cm) wide × 50" (127cm) long

SUPPLIES

- *4¼ yards (3.9m) of 45" (115cm) wide decorator fabric, such as muslin, chintz, or broadcloth*
- *1¼ yards (1.2m) of 45" (115cm) wide nonwoven pattern-duplicating material*
- *1 standard curtain rod*

STENCILING (optional)

- *Oiled stencil paper or stencil acetate*
- *Graphite paper for transferring the design*
- *Craft knife*
- *Two ½" (1.3cm) flat stencil brushes*
- *2 stencil paint creams, such as Stencil Magic (choose one light and one dark shade of the same color)*
- *Soap and water or turpentine to clean brushes, as directed by the paint manufacturer*
- *Fixative spray, such as Krylon*

CUTTING DIRECTIONS

All measurements include ½" (1.3cm) seam allowances.

Using the pattern-duplicating material, follow **Diagram 1** to create the swag and swag lining pattern.

Fold the decorator fabric along the crosswise grain, as shown in **Diagram 2,** and cut one swag and one swag lining.

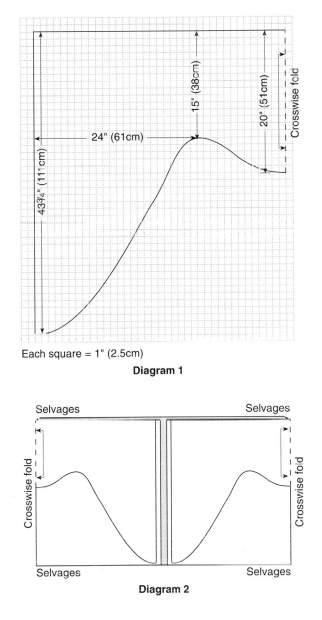

Each square = 1" (2.5cm)

Diagram 1

Diagram 2

SEWING DIRECTIONS

1 Joining the swag and the lining

With right sides together, pin the swag to the lining. Stitch the two sections together, leaving the upper edge open, as shown in **Diagram 3**. Trim the corners and clip the curves.

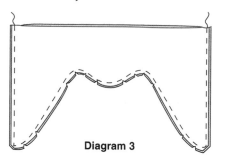

Diagram 3

Turn the swag right side out. Press. Machine baste ½″ (1.3cm) from the upper edges, as shown in **Diagram 4.**

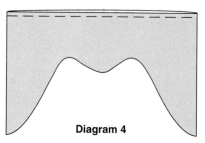

Diagram 4

2 **Making the header and rod pocket**

Referring to **Diagram 5,** press under ½″ (1.3cm) along the machine basting at the upper edge. Press under again 3″ (7.5cm). Stitch close to the first fold.

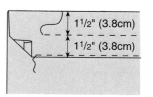

1½″ (3.8cm)

1½″ (3.8cm)

Diagram 5

Stitch again 1½″ (3.8cm) from the upper edge, forming a 1½″ (3.8cm) header and 1½″ (3.8cm) rod pocket.

✨ SEW SIMPLE

To achieve a crisply pressed lower edge, press the seam open first, before turning the swag right side out. To accommodate the seam's curved areas, use a tailor's ham as your pressing surface. No ham? The curved arms of an overstuffed chair, protected with a terry cloth towel, can be an effective substitute.

STENCILING DIRECTIONS

1 **Preparing the stencil**

Before you begin, review the information on page 127 in "Stenciling."

Using **Diagrams 6** and **7** on page 13, prepare the stencils for the bow and the ribbon as directed.

2 **Applying the design**

Fold the swag in half so that the sides match. Pin mark the center fold. Unfold the swag. Referring to **Diagram 8,** position the bow stencil so that the knot is on the center fold and the upper edges of the loops are midway between the bottom of the rod pocket and the bottom of the swag. Stencil the bow, using the lighter shade of paint for the lower part of the loops and the darker shade for the upper part of the loops.

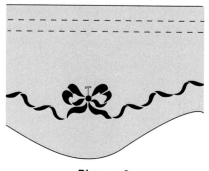

Diagram 8

Using the ribbon stencil, stencil along the curve of the swag to the lower ends, pivoting the stencil to match the curves, as necessary (see **Diagram 9**). Alternate the light and dark shades of the paint.

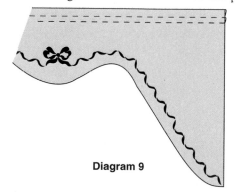

Diagram 9

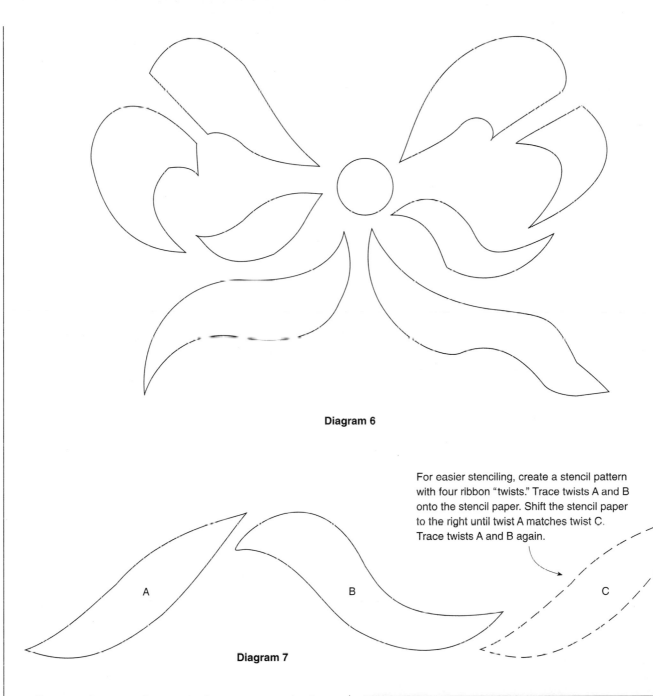

Diagram 6

For easier stenciling, create a stencil pattern with four ribbon "twists." Trace twists A and B onto the stencil paper. Shift the stencil paper to the right until twist A matches twist C. Trace twists A and B again.

A   B   C

Diagram 7

Following the manufacturer's directions, apply the fixative spray to the finished design.

INSTALLATION

Install the rod at the window and hang the swag, as shown in the photograph on page 10.

✦ DESIGN PLUS

For a completely different look, omit the stenciling in favor of an overall print. Be careful, however, when choosing a stripe or a one-way motif: This swag is cut crosswise, so any vertical motif will end up running horizontally on the finished treatment.

Little girls in particular will love this frilly valance, which sweeps across the top of the window like a graceful petticoat.

FEMININE FESTOON

Window Size:

36" (91.5cm) wide

SUPPLIES

- *1½ yards (1.4m) of 45" (115cm) wide decorator fabric, such as chintz, polished cotton, sateen, or broadcloth*
- *2¾ yards (2.6m) of 45" (115cm) wide contrasting decorator fabric (for the lining, rod covers, bows, and knots)*
- *1¼ yards (1.2m) of light- to medium-weight fusible interfacing*
- *1½ yards (1.4m) of 3½" (9cm) wide pregathered eyelet lace trim*
- *1½ yards (1.4m) of 45" (115cm) wide nonwoven pattern-duplicating material*
- *1 standard curtain rod*
- *One 2½" (6.3cm) wide continental rod*

Diagram 1

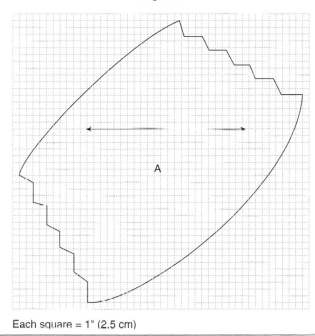

Each square = 1" (2.5 cm)

CUTTING DIRECTIONS

All measurements include ½" (1.3cm) seam allowances.

Using the pattern-duplicating material, create the valance pattern shown in **Diagram 1.**

From the decorator fabric, cut the following pieces, as shown in **Diagram 2:**

- *1 festoon (A)*
- *One 4½" × 37" (11.5cm × 94cm) casing (B)*

From the contrasting decorator fabric, cut the following pieces, using the patterns shown in **Diagram 3:**

- *Two 7½" × 45" (19cm × 115cm) rod covers (C)*
- *Four 5" × 45" (12.5cm × 115cm) bows with slanted ends (D)*
- *Two 4" × 5" (10cm × 12.5cm) knots (E)*

From the remaining contrasting fabric, cut one festoon (A), as shown in **Diagram 2.** This will be the festoon lining.

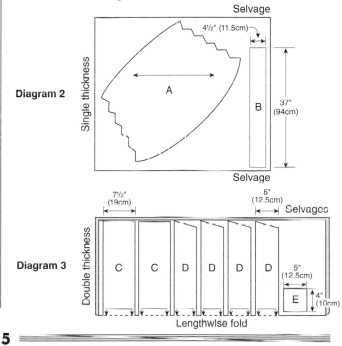

Diagram 2

Diagram 3

SEWING DIRECTIONS

1 Assembling the festoon

With right sides together, stitch the decorator festoon to the contrasting festoon lining along the lower edge, as shown in **Diagram 4.** Trim the seam.

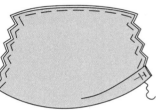

Diagram 4

Turn the festoon right side out and press the lower edge. Baste the layers together along the upper and side edges, as shown in **Diagram 5.**

Diagram 5

To shape the festoon, start on one side at the lower edge of the festoon. Referring to **Diagram 6,** make a soft fold along the edge at the first indentation.

Diagram 6

Bring the fold up to about ¼" (6mm) below the next indentation and pin in place at the side of the festoon. Repeat, making five pleats on each side of the festoon.

To check the shape and width of the festoon, pin it to the edge of an ironing board, as shown in **Diagram 7.** Adjust the pleats, as necessary, so that the folds are even and the festoon measures approximately 35½" (90cm) across the top. Remove the festoon from the ironing board. Baste the layers together across the top, as shown in **Diagram 8.**

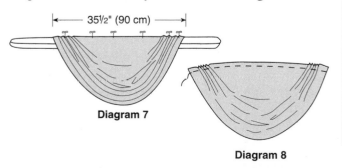

← 35½" (90 cm) →

Diagram 7

Diagram 8

2 Making the casing

Press under ¼" (6mm) along the ends of the casing. Press under again ½" (1.3cm). Stitch close to the first fold, as shown in **Diagram 9.** Fold the casing in half lengthwise, with wrong sides together, and press.

With right sides together, pin the casing to the festoon, as shown in **Diagram 10.** If necessary, ease the festoon to fit. Stitch. Press the casing up, away from the festoon.

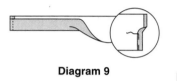

Diagram 9

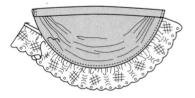

Diagram 10

3 Applying the trim

Pin the eyelet trim in place along the lower curved edge of the festoon, lapping the edge of the festoon over the upper (gathered) edge of the trim and turning the ends of the trim under. Topstitch the trim along the seam, as shown in **Diagram 11.**

Diagram 11

🧵 SEW SIMPLE

To obtain a secure bond between fabric and fusible interfacing, apply the interfacing to the wrong side of the fabric, following the interfacing manufacturer's directions. Repeat the fusing process on the right side of the fabric.

4 Making the rod cover

With right sides together, stitch the two rod cover pieces together to form the center front seam. Press the seam to one side.

Press under ¼" (6mm) along the ends of the cover. Press under again ½" (1.3cm). Stitch close to the first fold, as shown in **Diagram 12.**

Diagram 12

Fold the cover in half lengthwise, with right sides together, and stitch the seam, as shown in **Diagram 13.** Trim the seam. Turn the cover right side out and press.

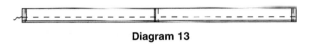

Diagram 13

5 Making the bows

Apply fusible interfacing to the wrong side of two bow pieces.

With right sides together, stitch one interfaced bow piece to one plain bow piece. Leave an opening in the center large enough for turning. Trim the corners, as shown in **Diagram 14.**

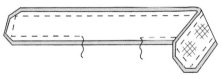

Diagram 14

Turn the seamed bow piece right side out and slip stitch the opening closed, following the directions on page 126 for slip stitching.

Fold the seamed bow piece in half crosswise. Measure 10" (25.5cm) from the fold and mark. Stitch across the bow at the marking. Refold the bow so that the center fold meets the stitching line, as shown in **Diagram 15.**

Diagram 15

Fold one knot piece in half lengthwise, right sides together, and stitch the seam, as shown in **Diagram 16.** Turn the knot piece right side out and press.

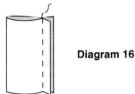

Diagram 16

Referring to **Diagram 17,** pleat the bow at the center to form two horizontal folds. Wrap the knot piece around the center of the bow and hand sew the edges together on the back of the bow.

Diagram 17

Repeat for a second bow and knot.

INSTALLATION

Install the continental rod at the top of the window frame. Install the standard rod behind the continental rod. Referring to **Diagram 18,** hang the festoon on the standard rod. Slip the rod cover over the continental rod. Pin the bows in place at the corners of the continental rod.

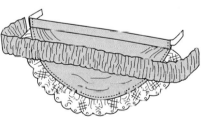

Diagram 18

✤ DESIGN PLUS

To create a tailored version of this valance, omit the bows and substitute fringe or pleated trim for the gathered lace.

This pretty valance provides a graceful counterpoint to shutters and mini-blinds without interfering with the amount of light that enters the room.

BUSTLE VALANCE

Window Size:

36" to 48" (91.5cm to 122cm) wide

SUPPLIES

- 5¼ yards (4.8m) of 45" to 60" (115cm to 153cm) wide decorator fabric, such as chintz, polished cotton, sateen, or broadcloth
- 2⅝ yards (2.4m) of contrasting covered piping
- 1¼ yards (1.2m) of 45" (115cm) wide nonwoven pattern-duplicating material
- One 2½" (6.3cm) wide continental rod

CUTTING DIRECTIONS

All measurements include ½" (1.3cm) seam allowances.

Using the pattern-duplicating material, create the valance pattern shown in **Diagram 1.**

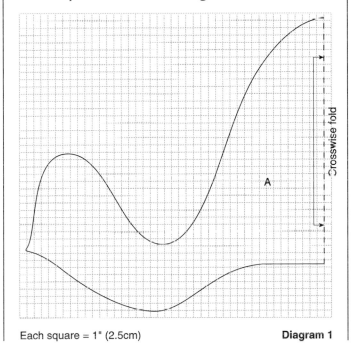

Each square = 1" (2.5cm)　　　　**Diagram 1**

From the decorator fabric, cut the following pieces, using the patterns shown in **Diagrams 2** and **3:**

- *1 valance (A)*
- *Two 13" × 41" (33cm × 104cm) center headers (B)*
- *Two 13" × 40⅛" (33cm × 102cm) side headers (C)*
- *Five 9" × 37" (23cm × 94cm) ruffle sections (D)*

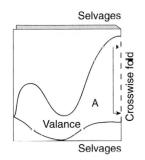

Diagram 2

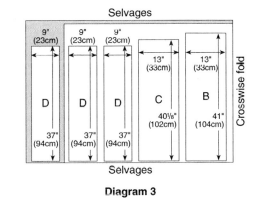

Diagram 3

SEWING DIRECTIONS

1 Making the header and rod pocket

With right sides together, stitch the two center header pieces together to form the center front seam. Press the seam open.

Stitch one side header to each end of the center header. Press the seams open.

Hem the sides by pressing under 1" (2.5cm), then 1" (2.5cm) again. Stitch close to the first fold, as shown in **Diagram 4.**

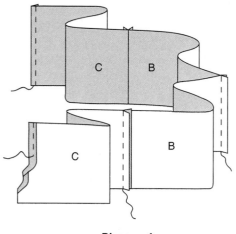

Diagram 4

With wrong sides together, fold the header in half lengthwise. Press. Stitch ⅝" (1.5cm) from the raw edges. Stitch again, 3" (7.5cm) from the pressed edge, as shown in **Diagram 5.**

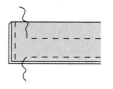

Diagram 5

2 Making the valance

On the right side of the valance, pin the piping to the lower, less curved edge, having the cord extend beyond the seam line and the lip within the seam allowance. Using the sewing machine zipper foot attachment, baste as close to the cord as possible without catching it, as shown in **Diagram 6.**

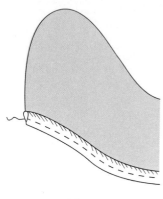

Diagram 6

Stitch the five ruffle sections together at the ends to form one long strip, as shown in **Diagram 7.** Press the seams open.

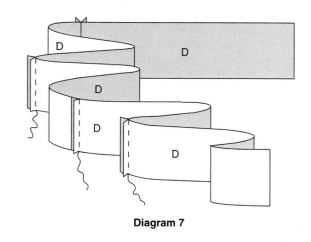

Diagram 7

🧵 SEW SIMPLE

When adding piping to a seam, here's how to make sure the basting stitches won't show on the finished project: Using the sewing machine zipper foot attachment, machine baste the piping to one section. Pin the two sections, with right sides together and the piped section on top. Baste, stitching over the first row of basting stitches. Then stitch the seam, crowding the zipper foot up next to the cord so that all of the basting stitches will be hidden in the seam allowance.

Referring to **Diagram 8,** fold the ruffle in half lengthwise, with wrong sides together. Press. Machine baste along the raw edge.

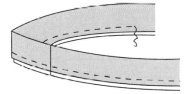

Diagram 8

Referring to **Diagram 9,** pin the ruffle to the lower edge of the valance, over the piping. Draw up the basting stitches, gathering the ruffle until the fullness is evenly distributed. Using the zipper foot attachment, baste and then stitch, crowding the stitches close to the cord. Trim the seam allowances; then machine finish the raw edges. Press the seam allowances toward the valance.

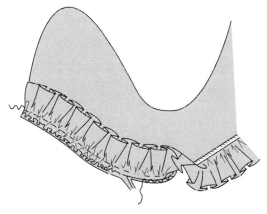

Diagram 9

3 Joining the header to the valance

Referring to **Diagram 10,** pin the header to the raw edge of the valance and ruffles, with right sides together. Match the centers and place the seams at the small dots. Ease to fit, clipping the header along the curves, if necessary. Stitch. Trim the seam allowances; then machine finish the raw edges. Press the seam allowances toward the valance.

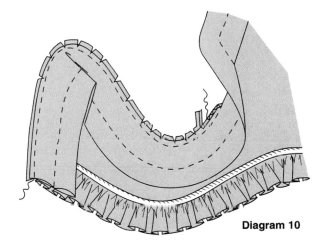

Diagram 10

INSTALLATION

Install the rod at the window and hang the valance, as shown in the photograph on page 18.

✦ DESIGN PLUS

To create the illusion of a slightly taller window, install the rod on the wall, slightly above the window frame.

A *double row of braid defines the gently curved edge of this handsome valance with contrasting lining.*

SCALLOPED VALANCE

Window Size:

30" to 45" (76cm to 115cm) wide

SUPPLIES

- 2⅝ yards (2.5m) of 45" to 60" (115cm to 153m) wide non-directional decorator fabric, such as chintz, polished cotton, sateen, or broadcloth

- 2⅝ yards (2.5m) of 45" to 60" (115cm to 153cm) wide contrasting decorator fabric

- 3⅝ yards (3.4m) of ½" (1.3cm) wide flexible braid trim

- 1½ yards (1.4m) of 45" (115cm) wide nonwoven pattern-duplicating material

- 1 standard curtain rod

✦ DESIGN PLUS

To make this valance from a fabric with a one-way design (for example, flowers that grow in one direction), you will need to cut and piece 1½ yards (1.4m) of decorator fabric before cutting out the valance. (Note: If your fabric has a repeat that must be matched, purchase extra fabric to accommodate for matching.)

- *Fold the fabric in half crosswise and cut into two sections. Fold one of these crosswise sections in half lengthwise and cut into two smaller sections. Keeping the selvage edges parallel, stitch the three sections together with the larger one in the center.*

- *Fold this long strip of fabric in half crosswise, matching the seam allowances. Cut out the valance, following the "Cutting Directions."*

CUTTING DIRECTIONS

All measurements include ½" (1.3cm) seam allowances.

Using the pattern-duplicating material, create the valance and valance lining pattern shown in **Diagram 1**.

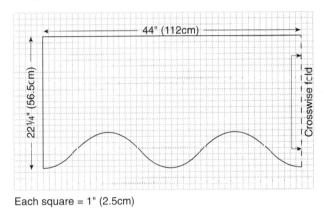

Each square = 1" (2.5cm)

Diagram 1

From the decorator fabric, cut one valance, as shown in **Diagram 2**.

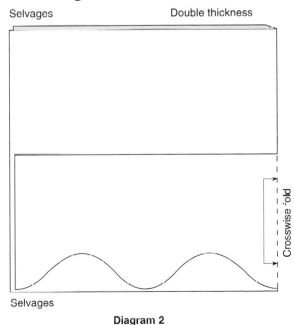

Diagram 2

From the contrasting decorator fabric, cut one valance lining, as shown in **Diagram 2.** Trim off 3″ (7.5cm) across the upper edge, as shown in **Diagram 3.**

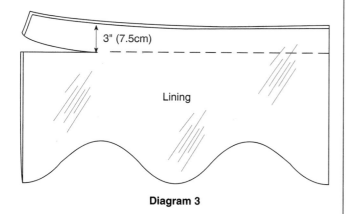

Diagram 3

SEWING DIRECTIONS

1 Assembling the valance

With right sides together, pin the valance to the valance lining, matching the side and lower edges, as shown in **Diagram 4.** Stitch along the side and lower edges. Trim the corners and clip the curves.

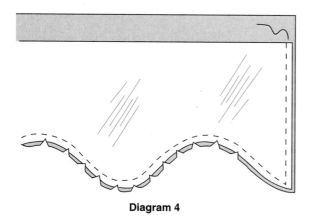

Diagram 4

Turn the valance right side out. Press, pressing under the side seam allowances at the upper edge, as shown in **Diagram 5.** Edge stitch along the side edges. Baste the upper edge of the lining in place.

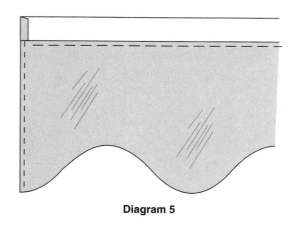

Diagram 5

2 Making the header and rod pocket

Referring to **Diagram 6,** press under ½″ (1.3cm) along the upper edge of the valance. Press under again 2½″ (6.3cm). Stitch close to the first fold.

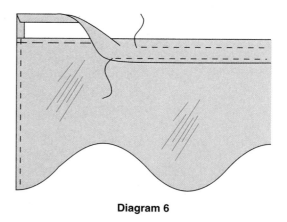

Diagram 6

Stitch again 1½″ (3.8cm) from the upper edge, forming a 1″ (2.5cm) header and a 1½″ (3.8cm) rod pocket.

3 Finishing the valance

Referring to **Diagram 7,** pin one row of flexible braid along the lower edge of the lining, wrapping the ends ½" (1.3cm) to the lining side. Stitch along both long edges of the braid. Apply a second row of braid directly above the first, slightly overlapping the long edges.

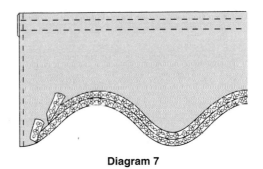

Diagram 7

🧵 SEW SIMPLE

To keep the braid from shifting during stitching, use a glue stick to baste it in place.

INSTALLATION

Install the rod at the window and hang the valance, as shown in the photograph on page 22.

This pretty pouf is the perfect way to add a bright touch of color to any room in the house.

POUF VALANCE

Window Size:

36" to 50" (91.5cm to 127cm) wide

SUPPLIES

- 2½ yards (2.3m) of 48" or 54" (122cm or 138cm) wide decorator fabric, such as chintz, polished cotton, or moiré
- 1 large café curtain rod
- Tissue paper or clear plastic dry cleaner bags (with no printing on them)

CUTTING DIRECTIONS

All measurements include ½" (1.3cm) seam allowances.

Cut two panels of fabric, each 43" (110cm) long × the width of the fabric.

✦ DESIGN PLUS

It's easy to adjust this valance to fit a larger window. A window that is 51" to 76" (130cm to 193cm) wide requires 3¾ yards (3.5m) of fabric, cut into three 43" (110cm) long panels. A window that is 77" to 102" (196cm to 259cm) wide requires 5 yards (4.6m) of fabric, cut into four 43" (110cm) long panels. Stitch the panels together, as in Step 1, to form one long section.

SEWING DIRECTIONS

1 Joining the panels

With right sides together, pin the panels of fabric together along one side edge. Stitch the seam and press it open, as shown in **Diagram 1.**

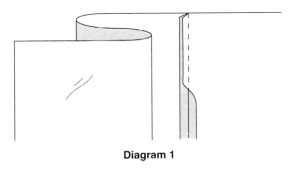

Diagram 1

2 Hemming the sides

Press under ½" (1.3cm) along the side edges of the panel. Press under again 1½" (3.8cm). Stitch close to the first fold, as shown in **Diagram 2.**

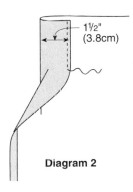

1½"
(3.8cm)

Diagram 2

3 Making the header and rod pocket

Referring to **Diagram 3,** fold the valance in half crosswise with wrong sides together. Machine baste the upper edges together. (Do not press the lower folded edge.)

Diagram 3

Referring to **Diagram 4,** press under ½″ (1.3cm) along the basted edge. Press under again 3″ (7.5cm). Stitch close to the first fold. Stitch again 3″ (7.5cm) below the first fold.

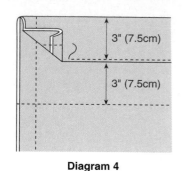

3″ (7.5cm)

3″ (7.5cm)

Diagram 4

INSTALLATION

Install the rod at the window and hang the valance, as shown in the photograph on page 26, distributing the gathers evenly across the window. To create the gently rounded pouf, insert loosely crumbled tissue paper or plastic dry cleaner bags between the layers.

🧵 SEW SIMPLE

Use a yardstick or broom handle to help push the tissue toward the center of the valance.

SWOOPS & SWAGS

This soft, flowing window treatment can be constructed entirely at the ironing board.

NO-SEW KNOTTED SWAG

Window Size:

36" to 48" (91.5cm to 122cm) wide

SUPPLIES

- *45" to 60" (115cm to 153cm) wide lightweight, non-directional decorator fabric with no obvious right or wrong side, such as broadcloth, voile, dotted swiss, or batiste**
- *Two 10-yard (9.2m) rolls of ¾" (2cm) wide paper-backed fusible web*
- *1 standard curtain rod*
- *1 tieback bracket*
- *Tape measure*
- *Masking tape*

*See the "Cutting Directions" for additional information.

CUTTING DIRECTIONS

To determine the length of the swag, refer to **Diagram 1.** Use masking tape to mark on each side of the window where you want the swags to end. Install the curtain rod at the top of the window. Use masking tape to secure one end of the tape measure to the end of the rod. Drape the tape across the window until it falls into the desired swag (A). Secure it to the other end of the rod with tape. Measure from each swag end to the rod (B and C).

Diagram 1

To determine the cutting length, add A + B + C + 48" (122cm).

To determine how many yards (meters) of fabric to purchase, divide the cutting length by 36" (91.5cm).

From the decorator fabric, cut the swag piece, using the pattern shown in **Diagram 2.** Trim along the diagonal lines.

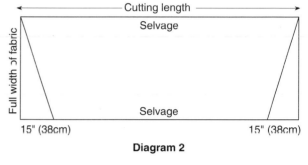

Diagram 2

FUSING DIRECTIONS

Hem all four sides of the swag, following the directions on page 126 for no-sew hemming.

INSTALLATION

Hang the swag at the window, as shown in the photograph, using the masking tape markings as length guides. Secure the swag to the rod at each corner with a half-knot. Loosely tie the longer end of the swag in a half-knot, adjusting the position of the knot until the proportion is pleasing. Install the tieback bracket to correspond to the knot; then loop the knot over the tieback bracket.

✦ DESIGN PLUS

If you need extra holding power, use nonrusting straight pins to secure the swag on the rod. Conceal the pins in the folds of the fabric.

This elegant window treatment is a simplified version of a true decorating classic.

TRADITIONAL SWAG & JABOTS

Window Size:

36" (91.5cm) wide × 40" to 60" (102cm to 153cm) long

SUPPLIES

- 3½ yards (3.3m) of 45" (115cm) wide non-directional decorator fabric, such as chintz, polished cotton, sateen, or broadcloth
- 4¼ to 7¼ yards (3.9m to 6.7m) of 45" (115cm) wide contrasting decorator fabric*
- 3¼ yards (3m) of 45" (115cm) wide nonwoven pattern-duplicating material
- 1 double curtain rod

*See the "Cutting Directions" for additional information.

CUTTING DIRECTIONS

All measurements include ½" (1.3cm) seam allowances.

Using the pattern-duplicating material, create the swag pattern shown in **Diagram 1** and the jabot pattern shown in **Diagram 2**. Note that there are three choices of jabot lengths. For an attractive proportion, choose a length that is shorter than the window length.

⊕ DESIGN PLUS

To change the look of this window treatment, rearrange the coordinating prints—make matching swag and jabots with contrasting lining or match the inside of each jabot to the swag.

The length of the jabot will determine how much contrasting fabric is required.

- *For a 35" (89cm) length, purchase 4¼ yards (3.9m).*
- *For a 53" (135cm) length, purchase 6¼ yards (5.8m).*
- *For a 59" (150cm) length, purchase 7¼ yards (6.7m).*

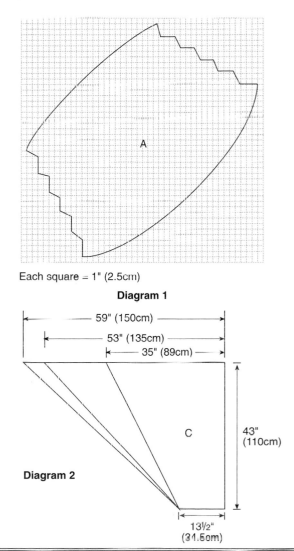

Each square = 1" (2.5cm)

Diagram 1

59" (150cm)
53" (135cm)
35" (89cm)

C

43" (110cm)

Diagram 2

13½" (31.5cm)

From the non-directional decorator fabric, cut the following pieces, using the patterns shown in **Diagram 3:**

- *2 swags (A)*
- *One 4½" × 37" (11.5cm × 94cm) swag casing (B)*

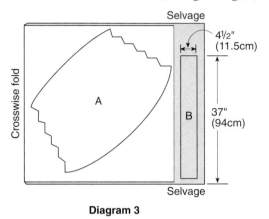

Diagram 3

From the contrasting fabric, cut the following pieces, using the patterns shown in **Diagram 4:**

- *4 jabots (C)*
- *Two 4½" × 12" (11.5cm × 30.5cm) jabot casings (D)*

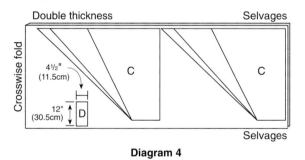

Diagram 4

SEWING DIRECTIONS

1 Assembling the swag

With right sides together, stitch the two swag pieces together along the lower edge, as shown in **Diagram 5.** Trim the seam allowances.

Turn the swag right side out and press the lower edge. Understitch the seam, following the directions on page 126 for understitching. Baste the layers together along the upper and side edges, as shown in **Diagram 6.**

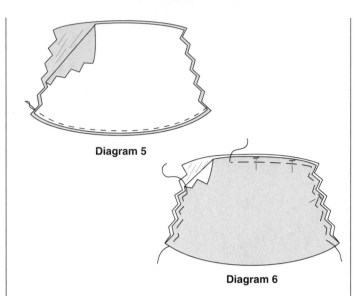

Diagram 5

Diagram 6

To shape the swag, start on one side at the lower edge of the swag. Referring to **Diagram 7,** make a soft fold along the edge at the first indentation. Bring the fold up to the next indentation and pin in place at the side of the swag. Repeat, making five pleats on each side of the swag.

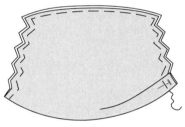

Diagram 7

To check the shape and width of the swag, pin it to the edge of an ironing board, as shown in **Diagram 8.** Adjust the pleats, as necessary, so that the folds are even and the swag measures approximately 35½" (90cm) across the top. Remove the swag from the ironing board. Baste the layers together across the top.

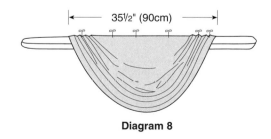

Diagram 8

2 Making the swag casing

Press under ¼" (6mm) along the ends of the swag casing. Press under again ½" (1.3cm). Stitch close to the first fold, as shown in **Diagram 9**. Fold the casing in half lengthwise, with wrong sides together, and press.

With right sides together, pin the casing to the swag, as shown in **Diagram 10**. If necessary, ease the swag to fit. Stitch. Press the casing up, away from the swag.

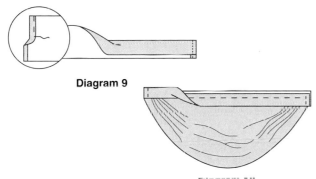

Diagram 9

Diagram 10

3 Making the jabots

With right sides together, stitch two jabot pieces together along the lower and side edges, as shown in **Diagram 11**. Leave the upper edges open. Trim the seams and corners. Turn the jabot right side out. Press. Pin the upper edges together. Repeat for the other two jabot pieces.

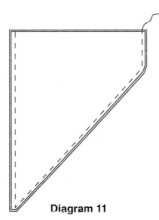

Diagram 11

Following **Diagram 12**, pin mark the solid and broken lines at the upper outside edge of one jabot.

Referring to **Diagram 13**, pleat the jabot by folding along the solid lines and bringing them to meet the broken lines. Start at the solid line closest to the inner (shortest) edge of the jabot. Secure the top of the pleats with pins. Repeat, making the second jabot a mirror image of the first.

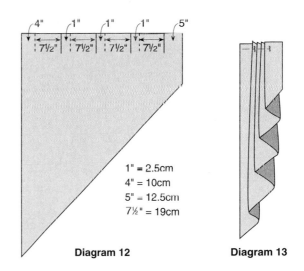

1" = 2.5cm
4" = 10cm
5" = 12.5cm
7½" = 19cm

Diagram 12   **Diagram 13**

Press under ½" (1.3cm) along each side edge of each jabot casing piece. Tuck each raw edge in to meet the crease. Press again. Stitch close to the second fold.

Fold each jabot casing in half lengthwise, with wrong sides together. Referring to **Diagram 14**, with right sides together, pin one casing to the top of each jabot. If necessary, adjust the depth of the folds so the jabot and casing match. Stitch. Press the casing up.

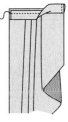

Diagram 14

INSTALLATION

Install the double curtain rod at the top of the window frame. Referring to **Diagram 15**, hang the swag on the back rod and the jabots on the front rod. Drape the swag over the jabots and arrange the folds, as shown in the photograph on page 32.

Diagram 15

⚙ SEW SIMPLE

To quickly distinguish solid lines from broken lines, mark one set with glass-head straight pins and the other set with plain straight pins.

Wreathed in style, this no-sew swag plus grapevine swag holders can be made in just a few hours.

SUPER SIMPLE SWAG

Window Size:

36" (91.5cm) wide × 50" (127cm) long

SUPPLIES

- *4 yards (3.7m) of 54" (138cm) wide non-directional decorator fabric*
- *Two 10-yard (9.2m) rolls of ¾" (2cm) wide strips of paper-backed fusible web*
- *2 tulip-shaped swag holders*
- *2 large safety pins*

WREATHS (optional)

- *Two 8" (20.5cm) diameter grapevine wreaths*
- *Floral materials to coordinate with your fabric (here, we used 6 stems of mini-rosebud sprays, 1 small package of baby's-breath, and 1 small package of dried mauve peppergrass)*
- *18-gauge wire*
- *2 nails or hooks to hang the wreaths*
- *Hot-glue gun and glue sticks*

CUTTING DIRECTIONS

From the decorator fabric, cut the swag piece, using the pattern shown in **Diagram 1.** Cut along the diagonal lines.

✦ DESIGN PLUS

If the window is wider than 36" (91.5cm), purchase fabric as follows:

- *For windows that are 36" to 45" (91.5cm to 115cm) wide, purchase 4¼ yards (3.9m).*
- *For windows that are 45" to 54" (115cm to 138cm) wide, purchase 4½ yards (4.2m).*
- *For windows that are 54" to 63" (138cm to 160cm) wide, purchase 4¾ yards (4.4m).*

FUSING DIRECTIONS

Hem all four sides of the swag, following the directions on page 126 for no-sew hemming.

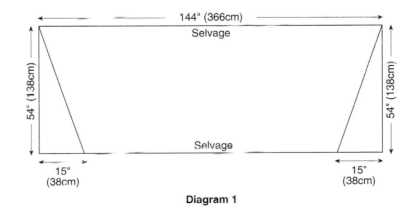

Diagram 1

🧵 SEW SIMPLE

As an alternative to fusing, the swag hems can be machine stitched.

WREATH DIRECTIONS

1 Decorating the wreaths

Starting at the middle on one side of one wreath, glue on three sprays of roses, arranging the sprays to extend continuously almost halfway around the wreath. Shape the roses and leaves to give them a natural look.

Cut the baby's-breath into 1½″ (3.8cm) pieces. Glue half of them around the roses and leaves on the wreath.

Cut the peppergrass into small clumps. Glue half of them around the flowers on the wreath.

Decorate the second wreath so that it is a mirror image of the first.

2 Attaching the hangers

Use the wire to make a secure loop on the back of each wreath at a point that corresponds to the midpoint of the rose sprays.

INSTALLATION

Install the swag holders at the upper corners of the window on the wall or window frame. Spread open the prongs of each holder.

Determine the center of the swag and mark with safety pins.

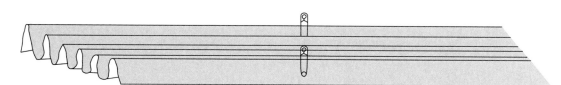

Diagram 2

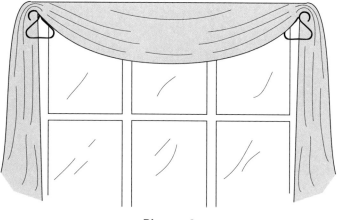

Diagram 3

Place the swag right side up on a large, flat surface. Beginning at the lower (shorter) edge, pleat the swag into accordion folds approximately 4″ (10cm) deep. Start and end with a full pleat, as shown in **Diagram 2**.

Center and drape the folded swag across the top of the window so that it rests on the top of the swag holders and the long, hemmed edges face the wall (see **Diagram 3**). Hold the top of the swag in place with one hand. With the other hand, pull the bottom fold down until the swag drapes to the desired depth at the center of the window and the swag holders are concealed underneath the fabric. Arrange the remaining folds along the center of the swag, keeping the upper edge straight. Adjust the swag tails, as shown in the photograph on page 36.

If necessary, use a few straight pins to secure the swag and tails around the swag holders.

Slip the wreaths up over the swag tails. Adjust each wreath so the fabric barely touches the bottom of the flowers. To secure each wreath, insert a nail or hook in the wall above the window to correspond to the wire loop on the back of each wreath.

⊕ DESIGN PLUS

For a holiday transformation, replace the floral wreaths with ones adorned with pinecones, holly berries, and other Christmas decorations.

This fool-the-eye window treatment is actually fashioned from easy-to-make components and cleverly installed on two separate rods.

TOGA SWAGS & JABOTS

Window Size:

36" to 48" (91.5cm to 122cm) wide

SUPPLIES

- *5½ yards (5.1m) of 45" to 60" (115cm to 153cm) wide non-directional decorator fabric, such as chintz, sateen, polished cotton, or broadcloth*
- *4½ yards (4.2m) of contrasting non-directional decorator fabric*
- *2¼ yards (2.1m) of 45" (115cm) wide nonwoven pattern-duplicating material*
- *1 standard curtain rod*
- *One 2½" (6.3cm) wide continental rod*
- *Water-soluble marking pen*

CUTTING DIRECTIONS

All measurements include ½" (1.3cm) seam allowances.

Using the pattern-duplicating material and following **Diagrams 1** and **2**, create the swag and swag lining pattern (A), the jabot and jabot lining pattern (B), and the jabot extension and jabot extension lining pattern (C).

🧵 SEW SIMPLE

When stitching problems occur, the sewing machine or the thread is often blamed, but the culprit is usually a bent or dull needle. Get in the habit of starting each project with a new needle.

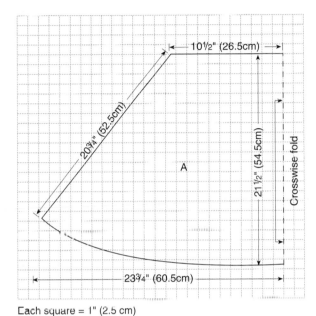

Each square = 1" (2.5 cm)

Diagram 1

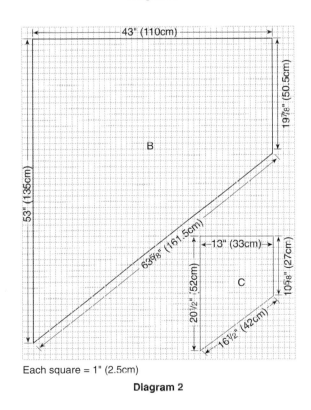

Each square = 1" (2.5cm)

Diagram 2

From the decorator fabric, cut the following pieces, as shown in **Diagram 3:**

- *2 swags (A)*
- *2 jabots (B)*
- *2 jabot extensions (C)*
- *Four 7⅜″ × 24¼″ (19cm × 61.5cm) swag headings (D)*
- *Two 5″ × 11″ (12.5cm × 28cm) jabot headings (E)*
- *Two 7⅜″ × 38″ (19cm × 96.5cm) spacers (F)*

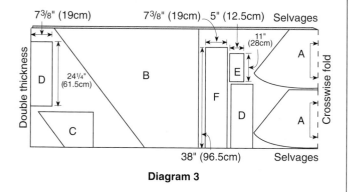

Diagram 3

From the contrasting decorator fabric, cut the following pieces, as shown in **Diagram 4:**

- *2 swag linings (A)*
- *2 jabot linings (B)*
- *2 jabot extension linings (C)*

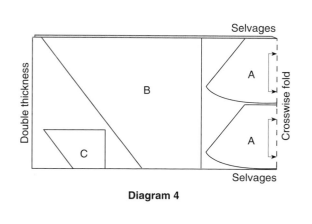

Diagram 4

SEWING DIRECTIONS

1 Making the swag headings

Press under 1″ (2.5cm) at the upper edge of one swag heading. Tuck the raw edge in to meet the crease. Stitch close to the second fold, as shown in **Diagram 5.** Repeat for the lower edge of the heading.

Fold the heading in half lengthwise with wrong sides together. Stitch ½″ (1.3cm) from the raw edges, as shown in **Diagram 6.**

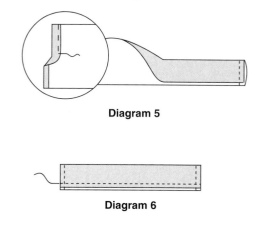

Diagram 5

Diagram 6

Repeat, making three more swag headings.

2 Assembling the swags

With right sides together, pin one swag to one swag lining. Stitch together along the upper and lower edges, as shown in **Diagram 7.** Turn the swag right side out and press.

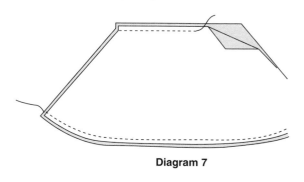

Diagram 7

Stitch one heading to each side edge of the swag, as shown in **Diagram 8**. Finish the seam allowances by zigzagging the edge or machine stitching ¼" (6mm) from the raw edges. Press the seam allowances toward the swag.

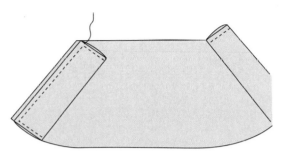

Diagram 8

Repeat, making the second swag.

3 Assembling the jabots

With right sides together, stitch one jabot to one jabot extension, matching the 19⅞" (50.5cm) edge of the jabot to the 20½" (52cm) edge of the jabot extension, as shown in **Diagram 9**. Press the seam open. Repeat, joining one jabot lining to one jabot extension lining.

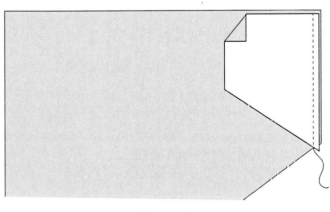

Diagram 9

With right sides together, stitch the jabot to the jabot lining, leaving the upper edge open, as shown in **Diagram 10**. Turn the jabot right side out and press. Baste the jabot and lining together along the upper edge.

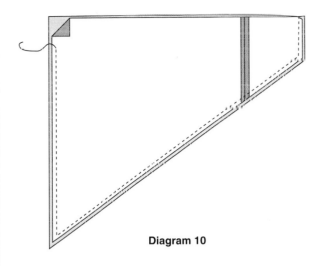

Diagram 10

Repeat, assembling the second jabot.

4 Pleating the jabots

Place one jabot faceup on a large, flat surface. Using the marking pen, measure and mark four parallel lines, as shown in **Diagram 11**. Pin or hand baste the layers together along these lines.

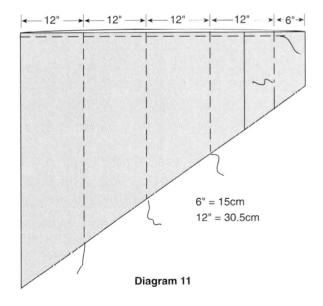

6" = 15cm
12" = 30.5cm

Diagram 11

Starting at the shortest edge of the jabot, fold along the first line and bring the fold in to meet the second line, as shown in **Diagram 12** on page 44. Pin along the upper edge, keeping the raw edges even.

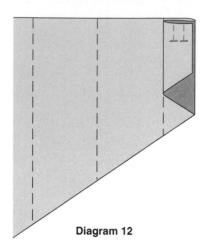

Diagram 12

In the same manner, fold along the second line and bring both folded edges in to meet the third marked line, as shown in **Diagram 13**. Continue in this manner until the entire jabot is folded, as shown in **Diagram 14**. Machine baste across the upper edge through all the layers. Remove the pins or the hand-basting stitches along the folds.

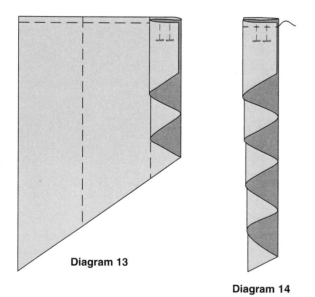

Diagram 13

Diagram 14

Repeat, pleating the second jabot in a mirror image of the first.

5 Finishing the jabots

Press under 1″ (2.5cm) at one short edge of one jabot heading. Tuck the raw edge in to meet the crease. Stitch close to the second fold. Repeat for the other short edge of the heading.

Fold the heading in half lengthwise with wrong sides together and press, as shown in **Diagram 15.**

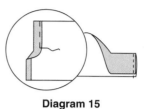

Diagram 15

Referring to **Diagram 16,** center and pin the heading to the upper edge on the right side of one jabot. Stitch; then finish the seam allowances by zigzagging the edge or machine stitching ¼″ (6mm) from the raw edges. Press the seam allowances toward the jabot.

Diagram 16

Repeat, finishing the second jabot.

✿ DESIGN PLUS

For a professional look, steam set the pleats before hanging the jabots. Place them on a flat, padded surface. Smooth out the pleats. Hold the iron several inches (centimeters) above each jabot and apply a generous amount of steam. Do not disturb the jabots until they are thoroughly cool and dry.

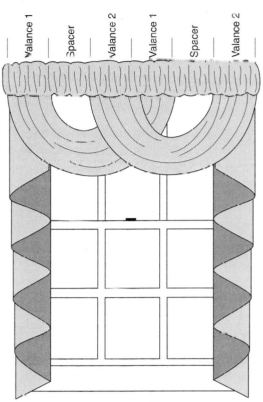

6 Making the spacers

Press under 1" (2.5cm) at one short edge of one spacer. Tuck the raw edge in to meet the crease. Stitch close to the second fold. Repeat for the other short edge of the spacer.

Fold the spacer in half lengthwise with right sides together. Stitch along the long edge, as shown in **Diagram 17.** Turn the spacer right side out. Press.

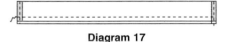

Diagram 17

Repeat, making the second spacer

INSTALLATION

Install the rods on the wall above the window, as shown in the photograph on page 40, so that the standard curtain rod is behind the continental rod. Hang the jabots on the standard curtain rod. Hang valance 1, valance 2, and the spacers on the continental rod in the sequence shown in **Diagram 18.**

Diagram 18

🧵 SEW SIMPLE

Nonwoven pattern-duplicating material is printed with an accurate 1" (2.5cm) graph. It is useful for duplicating, altering, and scaling up patterns. Brand names include Pellon Tru-Grid and Red Dot Tracer.

Soft and airy, this window treatment conjures up visions of wide green lawns, lazy summer days, and gracious southern hospitality.

VIRGINIA SWAG

Window Size:

24" to 36" (61cm to 91.5cm) wide

SUPPLIES

- *45" to 60" (115cm to 153cm) wide light-to medium-weight decorator fabric, such as broadcloth, moiré, voile, lace, or chintz**
- *2-cord shirring tape**
- *1 café curtain rod*
- *Tape measure*
- *Masking tape*
- *Dressmaker's chalk or water-soluble marking pen*

*See the "Cutting Directions" and Step 3 of the "Sewing Directions" for additional information.

CUTTING DIRECTIONS

All measurements include ½" (1.3cm) seam allowances.

To determine the length of the window treatment, install the rod at the top of the window. Measure from the top of the rod to the desired length (usually to the bottom of the windowsill or to the floor).

To determine the cutting length, add 5½" (14cm) to the desired length.

To determine how many yards (meters) of fabric to purchase, divide the cutting length by 36" (91.5cm). Add ¼ yard (0.3m) for the tie.

From the decorator fabric, cut one panel piece equal to the cutting length of the window treatment by the width of the fabric. Cut one tie piece 5" (12.5cm) long × the width of the fabric.

SEWING DIRECTIONS

1 Hemming the panel

Referring to **Diagram 1,** press under ½" (1.3cm) along each side edge of the panel piece. Tuck the raw edge in to meet the crease. Press again. Stitch close to the second fold. Use the same technique to hem the lower edge.

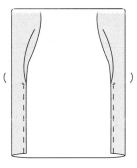

Diagram 1

2 Making the header and rod pocket

Referring to **Diagram 2,** press under ½" (1.3cm) along the upper edge of the panel piece. Press under again 3" (7.5cm). Stitch close to the first fold. Stitch again 1½" (3.8cm) from the upper edge.

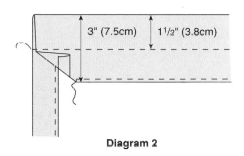

3" (7.5cm) 1½" (3.8cm)

Diagram 2

3 Creating the swag

Referring to **Diagram 3,** drape a tape measure across the top of the window, between the ends of the rod, until it falls into the desired swag. Use masking tape to secure the ends. This measurement plus 1″ (2.5cm) is the swag measurement.

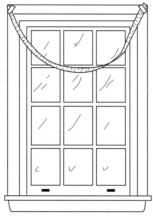

Diagram 3

Working on the wrong side of the panel, as shown in **Diagram 4,** start at the upper edge of the panel and measure down along one side a distance equal to the swag measurement and mark it, using the chalk or marking pen. Next, draw a diagonal line from the opposite corner, just below the rod pocket, to this mark. Begin the diagonal line 1″ (2.5cm) in from the side edge, below the rod pocket. Purchase an amount of 2-cord shirring tape

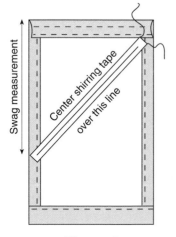

Diagram 4

equal to the length of this diagonal line. Center the shirring tape over the diagonal line. Stitch along both long edges of the tape. Tie the cords together securely at the bottom of the swag measurement. Leave the cords free at the top of the panel for pulling.

4 Making the tie

Fold the tie piece in half lengthwise, with right sides together. Stitch the long edges together, as shown in **Diagram 5.**

Diagram 5

Turn the tie right side out. Press. Tuck in the ends, as shown in **Diagram 6,** and slip stitch the openings closed, following the directions on page 126 for slip stitching.

Diagram 6

🧵 SEW SIMPLE

A glue stick is a great no-pins way to hold the shirring tape securely in place for stitching. After applying the glue, let it dry for a few minutes before stitching. Otherwise, you may gum up your sewing machine needle.

Fold the tie in half crosswise to locate the center. Position the tie on the back of the panel, following the diagonal line of shirring tape, as shown in **Diagram 7**. Hand sew the center of the tie to the back of the rod pocket, just above the shirring tape. Be careful not to sew the rod pocket closed.

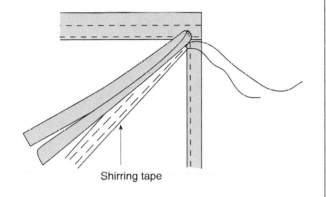

Shirring tape

Diagram 7

INSTALLATION

Pull up the shirring cords as tight as possible and tie them securely. Hang the panel on the rod; then install the rod at the window. Wrap the tie around the swag and fasten it with a square knot, as shown in the photograph on page 46. Arrange the folds of the swag to achieve the desired look.

✦ DESIGN PLUS

If your window is more than 36" (91.5cm) wide—or if you have two windows side by side— why not frame them with a pair of Virginia swags? Reverse the direction of the shirring tape on one of the swags and install both swags on a single rod.

A *clever plastic frame is the simple secret behind this no-sew window dressing.*

NO-SEW BUTTERFLY SWAG

Window Size:

36" (91.5cm) wide × 40" to 60" (102cm to 153cm) long. The length of the window treatment is based on a room with 8' (244cm) ceilings and windows that are approximately 12" (30.5cm) from the ceiling. The ends of the swag puddle approximately 8" (20.5cm) on the floor.

SUPPLIES

- *11⅛ yards (10.3m) of 60" (153cm) wide decorator fabric, such as chintz, polished cotton, sateen, or sheeting*
- *Three 10-yard (9.3m) rolls of ¾" (2cm) wide paper-backed fusible web*
- *One 36" (91.5cm) long Butterfly Ladder*
- *2 yards (1.9m) of nylon cable cord*
- *18 small ribbon roses*
- *4 cup hooks*
- *Hot-glue gun and glue sticks*
- *Masking tape*

CUTTING DIRECTIONS

Use the full length of the decorator fabric for the swag panel.

FUSING DIRECTIONS

1 Hemming the swag

Hem all four edges of the swag panel, using the fusible web and following the directions on page 126 for no-sew hemming.

2 Creating the balloon top

Fold the swag panel in half crosswise and pin mark the center.

Open the panel and place it right side up on a flat surface. Place the Butterfly Ladder on top, matching the center of the ladder to the center of the swag panel, as shown in **Diagram 1.**

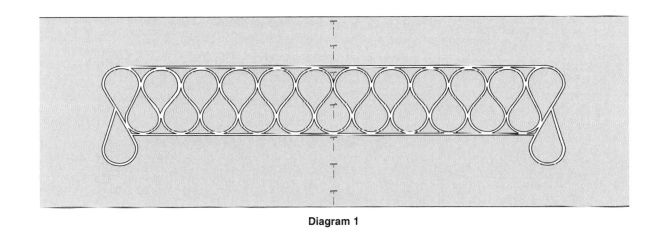

Diagram 1

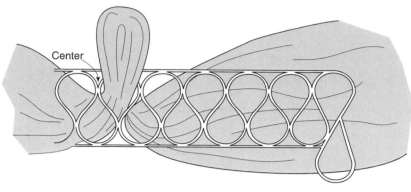

Center

Diagram 2

Pull the fabric up through the upper right center ring, using 18″ to 20″ (45.5cm to 51cm) of the fabric to form a loop, as shown in **Diagram 2.** Continue across the upper right side of the ladder, pulling the fabric through the rings to make four more loops. Use only the upper row of rings and make all the loops the same size. Repeat, making loops across the upper left side of the ladder until there are ten loops in all. If necessary, adjust the size of the loops until both swag ends are the same length.

Fan out each loop to create a balloon effect.

Pull the swag ends up through the end loops of the ladder.

🧵 SEW SIMPLE

If the selvage edges look the same as the rest of the fabric, there's no need to hem the side edges of the panel.

✤ DESIGN PLUS

To keep the fabric loops and poufs from sagging, lightly stuff them with polyester fiberfill.

INSTALLATION

Install a cup hook at each upper corner of the window, on the wall or window frame. Hang the ladder on the hooks.

Determine the location of the side poufs by tying a piece of cable cord around each curtain. Adjust the poufs to create a pleasing proportion, allowing some of the swag ends to puddle on the floor. Temporarily secure the cords to the window frame with bits of masking tape. Attach the two remaining cup hooks to the window frame at the desired locations. Hook the cords onto the cup hooks. Conceal the cord tails behind the swag ends.

Scatter and glue the ribbon roses across the top and on the sides of the window treatment, as shown in the photograph on page 50.

SHADES

This lined Roman shade fits snugly inside the window, protecting the room from hot summer sunshine and cold winter breezes.

ROMAN SHADE

Window Size:

36" to 56" (91.5cm to 143cm) wide × not more than 50" (127cm) long. To customize for a longer window, see "Sew Simple" before buying supplies.

SUPPLIES

- *1½ yards (1.4m) of decorator fabric, such as chintz, polished cotton, sateen, or broadcloth**
- *1½ yards (1.4m) of lining fabric, such as polished cotton or broadcloth**
- *Ring tape**
- *Nylon cable cord**
- *1 mounting board**
- *1 weight rod**
- *Screw eyes**
- *1 window cleat*
- *2 angle irons and mounting screws*
- *1 weighted shade pull*
- *Clear-drying craft glue*
- *Staple gun and staples*

*See "Cutting Directions" for more information.

CUTTING DIRECTIONS

All measurements include ½" (1.3cm) seam allowances.

Referring to **Diagram 1,** measure the window from side to side for the inside width (A) and from top to bottom for the inside length (B).

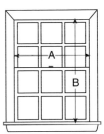

Diagram 1

Purchase one 1" × 2" (2.5cm × 5cm) mounting board that is equal to the window's inside width.

Purchase one weight rod that is ½" (1.3cm) shorter than the window's inside width.

Consult the chart below to determine the width of decorator fabric, number of rows and amount of ring tape, amount of nylon cord, and number of screw eyes, as determined by the inside width of the window.

From the decorator fabric, cut one panel that is 4" (10cm) wider than the inside width and 3" (7.5cm) longer than the inside length of the window. Mark the centers at the upper and lower edges.

From the lining fabric, cut one panel that is 2" (5cm) narrower than the inside width and 3" (7.5cm) longer than the inside length of the window. Mark the centers at the upper and lower edges.

INSIDE WIDTH OF WINDOW (A)	FABRIC WIDTH	ROWS OF RING TAPE	AMOUNT OF RING TAPE	AMOUNT OF NYLON CORD	NUMBER OF SCREW EYES
36" (91.5cm)	45" to 60" (115cm to 153cm)	4	6 yards (5.5m)	15 yards (13.9m)	4
37" to 41" (94cm to 104cm)	45" to 60" (115cm to 153cm)	5	7½ yards (6.9m)	18¾ yards (17.4m)	5
42" to 50" (107cm to 127cm)	54" to 60" (138cm to 153cm)	5	7½ yards (6.9m)	18¾ yards (17.4m)	5
51" to 56" (130cm to 143cm)	60" (153cm)	6	9⅛ yards (8.5m)	22⅞ yards (21.2m)	6

SEWING DIRECTIONS

1 Attaching the lining

With right sides together, pin the lining panel to the decorator fabric panel along the side edges, as shown in **Diagram 2**. Match the upper and lower edges. (Note: The lining will be narrower than the decorator fabric.) Stitch the side seams. Trim the seams. Press the seams toward the lining.

Turn the shade right side out. Match the centers so that the decorator fabric folds back 1" (2.5cm) on each side. Press.

Turn the shade inside out. Match the centers at the upper and lower edges. Pin the lower edges together. Stitch across the lower edges, as shown in **Diagram 3**. Turn the shade right side out again. Press the lower edge.

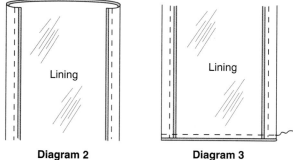

Diagram 2   **Diagram 3**

🧵 SEW SIMPLE

If the window's inside length (B), as shown in Diagram 1 on page 55, is more than 50" (127cm), you will need to increase the amount of decorator fabric, lining, ring tape, and nylon cord.

- *Purchase enough decorator fabric and lining to equal the window's inside length plus 4" (10cm).*
- *To determine how much ring tape to purchase, multiply the number of rows of tape, as indicated in the chart on page 55, by the length of the panel of decorator fabric.*
- *To determine how much nylon cord to purchase, multiply the amount of ring tape by 2.5.*

2 Hemming the upper and lower edges

Tuck the upper edges in ½" (1.3cm). Edge stitch, as shown in **Diagram 4**.

On the lining side, press the lower edge up 2" (5cm). Stitch.

Diagram 4

3 Attaching the ring tape

On the lining side, pin one row of ring tape along each side edge. Starting at the lower edge, place each row so that the bottom ring is just above the hem stitching and there is a 4" (10cm) tail of tape below. Add two, three, or four more rows of tape, evenly spaced in between. (The total number of rows is determined by the window width and is listed in the chart on page 55.) The rings should line up across the shade, as shown in **Diagram 5**. To make room for the mounting board, remove any rings that are within 3" (7.5cm) of the upper edge of the shade.

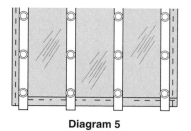

Diagram 5

Referring to **Diagram 6,** tuck each row end under to form a 1½" (3.8cm) loop below the bottom ring at the lower edge of the shade. Using a sewing machine zipper foot attachment, stitch down one side of each row to the bottom of the last ring, across the row, and up the other side.

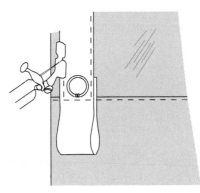

Diagram 6

4 **Rigging the shade**

Referring to **Diagram 7,** staple the top of the shade to the mounting board.

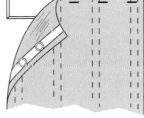

Diagram 7

Referring to **Diagram 8,** place the shade, lining side up, on a large, flat surface. Attach screw eyes to the back of the board to correspond with the rows of ring tape. Tie the nylon cord to one bottom ring. Secure the knot with a bit of glue. Thread the cord up through the remaining rings and across the top of the shade through the screw eyes to one corner. Trim the excess cord so that it is even with the lower edge of the shade. Repeat

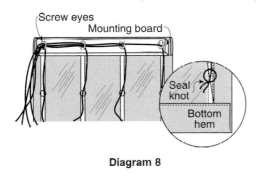

Screw eyes
Mounting board
Seal knot
Bottom hem

Diagram 8

for all of the rows of ring tape, running all of the cords through the screw eyes in the same direction.

Pull on the cords to form soft pleats. Insert the weight rod through the loops at the bottom of the shade.

INSTALLATION

Referring to **Diagram 9,** use the angle irons to install the mounting board like a shelf at the inside top of the window.

Diagram 9

Release the shade to its full length and tie all of the cords together outside the last screw eye. Apply glue to the center of the knot. When the glue has dried, cut off all but one cord. Attach the weighted shade pull to the end of the cord. Attach the cleat to the inside edge of the window frame about halfway down the window. Loop the cord around the cleat to hold the shade at the desired height.

✦ DESIGN PLUS

For a smooth, professional look, steam set the pleats before installing the shade. With the shade in the "up" position, smooth and straighten the folds. Apply steam generously. Let the shade dry thoroughly before releasing the pleats.

Light gently filters into the room, courtesy of this stationary shade exquisitely fashioned from a wide panel of lace.

LACE BALLOON SHADE

Window Size:

36" to 48" (91.5cm to 122cm) wide × 40" to 60" (102cm to 153cm) long

SUPPLIES

- *2⅛ yards (2m) of 72" (183cm) wide lace fabric*
- *12 yards (11m) of nylon cable cord*
- *One 2½" (6.3cm) wide continental rod*
- *1 window cleat*
- *Thirty-six ½" (1.3cm) plastic rings*
- *Water-soluble marking pen*
- *Clear-drying craft glue*

VALANCE (optional)

- *1 small bunch of twigs—approximately 10 to 12 pieces, each about 24" (61cm) long*
- *Floral materials to coordinate with your fabric (here, we used 1 small bunch of baby eucalyptus, 9 silk roses with buds, and 1 stem of baby's-breath)*
- *1½ yards (1.4m) of 1½" (39mm) wide wire-edge ribbon*
- *28-gauge wire*
- *Hot-glue gun and glue sticks*
- *Hook for hanging the valance*

CUTTING DIRECTIONS

From the lace fabric, cut one 70" (178cm) long panel. The selvage edges will be the side edges of the curtain.

SEWING DIRECTIONS

1 Hemming the lower edge

Press under 2" (5cm) along the lower edge of the lace panel. Tuck the lower edge in to meet the crease. Press again. Stitch close to the second fold, as shown in **Diagram 1.**

Diagram 1

2 Making the rod pocket

Press under ½" (1.3cm) along the upper edge of the panel. Press under again 3" (7.5cm). Stitch close to the first fold, as shown in **Diagram 2.**

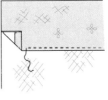

Diagram 2

🧵 SEW SIMPLE

If your lace has a very open weave, machine stitch vertical strips of sheer tricot seam binding, such as Seams Great, over the placement marks before attaching the rings.

3 Attaching the rings

Divide the panel into three equal spaces by drawing a vertical line 24" (61cm) in from each side on the wrong side of the fabric. Use the marking pen and refer to **Diagram 3.**

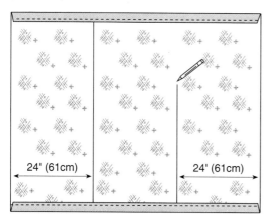

24" (61cm)   24" (61cm)

Diagram 3

Referring to **Diagram 4,** mark for the ring placement along each vertical line and 1" (2.5cm) in from each side edge. Make the first marks at the upper edge of the bottom hem. Continue marking every 5" (12.5cm) until there are eight marks at each side and on each line. Check to be sure the marks line up horizontally across the panel. Mark again along the lower edge of the rod casing at each vertical line and 1" (2.5cm) in from each side edge.

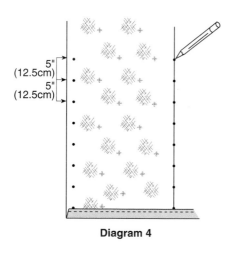

5"
(12.5cm)
5"
(12.5cm)

Diagram 4

Hand sew or machine stitch one ring at each mark, as shown in **Diagram 5.** To apply the rings by machine, set the machine for a zigzag stitch wide enough to go over the ring and a "0" stitch length.

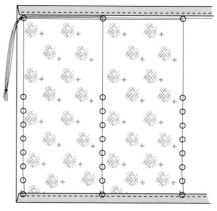

Diagram 5

4 Rigging the shade

Referring to **Diagram 6,** tie the nylon cable cord to one bottom ring. Secure the knot with a drop of glue. Thread the cord up through the remaining rings and across the top of the shade through the rings to one corner. Bring the cord down the side to half the length of the shade. Cut off the excess cord. Repeat for the remaining vertical rows of rings, running all the cords in the same direction across the top of the shade. Loosely tie the cords together at the top corner ring and at the cut ends.

Diagram 6

VALANCE DIRECTIONS

1 Making the base

Divide the twigs into two equal groups. Place the two groups so the stems overlap about 8″ (20.5cm). Intertwine them at the overlap and secure by wrapping with the 28-gauge wire in two or three places.

2 Applying the dried flowers

Cut the eucalyptus into 1½″ to 3″ (3.8cm to 7.5cm) pieces. Measure 5″ (12.5cm) out in both directions from the center of the twigs. Distribute and glue the eucalyptus within this 10″ (25.5cm) section of the twig valance.

Glue one rose at the center of the valance. Distribute and glue the other roses among the eucalyptus.

Cut small clumps of baby's-breath. Glue them in place around the roses and eucalyptus.

3 Making the bow

Fold the ribbon in half crosswise and pinch the tails together to form a 2″ (5cm) diameter loop. Glue the base of the loop to the valance, right below the center rose. Make another 2″ (5cm) loop on each side of the first one and glue in place. Twist the remaining ribbon through the twigs, as shown in the photograph on page 58, and glue in place. Cut the tail ends on an angle.

INSTALLATION

Install the rod at the top of the window frame. Hang the shade on the rod. Adjust the cords until the shade is at the desired length, as shown in **Diagram 7.** Reknot the cords at the corner and at the cut ends. Secure each knot with a drop of glue. Knot the cords together every 5″ (12.5cm) between the corner knot and the end knot.

Attach the cleat in the desired position at the side of the window frame. Wrap the cords around the cleat.

Install the hook at the center of the window, just above the shade. Hang the valance on the hook.

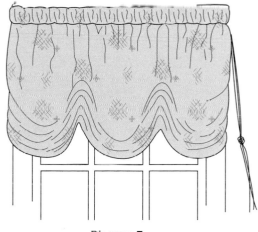

Diagram 7

*I*ron-on shade backing and an eye-catching fabric transform the utilitarian roller shade into an exciting fashion statement.

ROLLER SHADE

Window Size:

36″ to 40″ (91.5cm to 102cm) wide × 50″ (127cm) long. To customize for a longer or shorter window, see "Sew Simple" before purchasing supplies.

SUPPLIES

- 1¾ yards (1.7m) of 45″ to 60″ (115cm to 153cm) wide decorator fabric, such as chintz, broadcloth, or canvas
- 1¾ yards (1.7m) of iron-on shade backing
- Brackets, roller, and slat from a new or old shade
- T-square
- Liquid ravel preventer, such as Fray Check
- Masking tape
- Staple gun and staples or clear plastic tape
- Decorative shade pull or clear plastic shade grip

CUTTING DIRECTIONS

Referring to **Diagram 1,** measure across the window from side to side for the inside width (A) and from top to bottom for the inside length (B).

From the decorator fabric, cut one panel that is 3″ (7.5cm) wider than the inside width and 12″ (30.5cm) longer than the inside length, as shown in **Diagram 2.**

From the shade backing, cut a panel that is the same size as the decorator fabric panel.

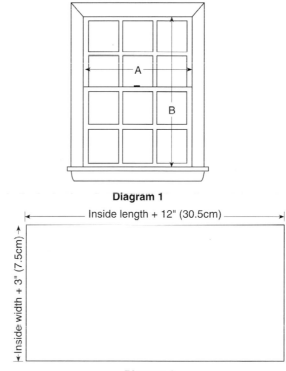

Diagram 1

Inside length + 12″ (30.5cm)

Inside width + 3″ (7.5cm)

Diagram 2

SEW SIMPLE

Shorter windows call for less fabric; longer windows require more. If the window's inside length is less than 45″ (115cm) or more than 50″ (127cm), purchase enough of the decorator fabric and the iron-on shade backing to cut panels equal to the inside length plus 12″ (30.5cm).

SEWING DIRECTIONS

1 **Fusing the shade**

Working on a long, flat surface, unroll the shade backing and place it fusible side up. Note any special instructions that come with it.

Place the decorator fabric, right side up, on top of the backing, as shown in **Diagram 3.** Remove any loose threads that may be sandwiched between the decorator fabric and the backing. Fuse the backing to the fabric, following the backing manufacturer's directions. Fuse from the center out toward the edges. Let the shade cool completely.

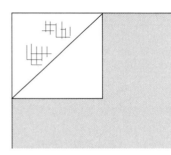

Diagram 3

Measure the length of the shade roller, from end to end, as shown in **Diagram 4.** Do not include the pin projections. Trim the width of the shade to equal the length of the roller. Square off both ends of the shade, using a T-square so all the corners are perfect right angles. Seal the long edges of the shade with liquid ravel preventer.

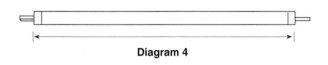

Diagram 4

2 Making the slat pocket

Turn under 1¼" (3.2cm) at the lower edge of the shade. Stitch close to the cut edge, as shown in **Diagram 5.**

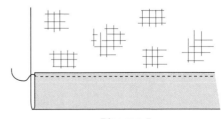

Diagram 5

SEW SIMPLE

For a no-sew shade, use staples instead of stitching to secure the cut edge of the slat pocket. Glue ribbon or braid in place on the front of the shade to conceal the staples.

Insert the slat in the pocket at the lower edge of the shade, as shown in **Diagram 6.**

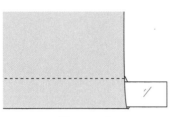

Diagram 6

3 Finishing the shade

Align the guideline on the roller with the upper edge of the shade. If the roller has no guideline, draw a straight line from one end to the other. Attach the upper edge of the shade to the roller, as shown in **Diagram 7.** For a wood or cardboard roller, temporarily attach the shade with masking tape; then use a staple gun and very short staples to permanently secure it. For a metal roller, use clear plastic tape to permanently attach the shade.

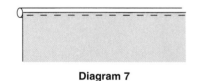

Diagram 7

DESIGN PLUS

If there are no plans for a top treatment, such as a cornice or valance, to conceal the top of the shade, be sure to attach the shade so it falls from the front of the roller. Install the brackets at the top of the window so that the flat pin will be on the right as you face the window.

INSTALLATION

Install the shade at the top of the window, as shown in the photograph on page 62. Attach a shade pull or shade grip at the center bottom of the shade.

⊕ DESIGN PLUS

Although a fabric shade can stand on its own, it can also be a beautiful companion to many other window treatments, such as the Scalloped Valance on page 22, the Traditional Swag & Jabots on page 32, and the Swoop-Top Curtains on page 108.

This gently billowing shade is adaptable to almost any decor, from feminine to formal, country to classic.

CLOUD SHADE

Window Size:

36" to 60" (91.5cm to 153cm) wide × 50" (127cm) long

CUTTING DIRECTIONS

All measurements include ½" (1.3cm) seam allowances.

Referring to **Diagram 1,** measure the outside width of the window (A).

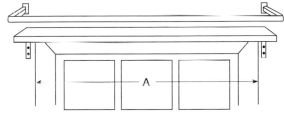

Diagram 1

Purchase enough 4-cord shirring tape to equal four times the window's outside width.

Purchase one ½" (1.3cm) diameter wood dowel that is equal to the window's outside width plus 1" (2.5cm).

Purchase one ½" × 1¾" (1.3cm × 4.5cm) mounting board that is equal to the window's outside width plus 1" (2.5cm).

Consult the chart below to determine the width of the decorator fabric and lining, number of rows and amount of ring tape, amount of nylon cord, and number of screw eyes.

Referring to **Diagram 1,** use the two angle irons to center and install the mounting board like a shelf

OUTSIDE WIDTH OF WINDOW (A)	WIDTH OF DECORATOR FABRIC AND LINING	ROWS OF RING TAPE	AMOUNT OF RING TAPE	AMOUNT OF NYLON CABLE CORD	NUMBER OF SCREW EYES
36" to 45" (91.5cm to 115cm)	45" to 60" (115cm to 153cm)	6	14 yards (13m)	3½ yards (29.3m)	12
46" to 60" (117cm to 153cm)	60" (153cm)	8	18½ yards (17.2m)	42 yards (39m)	16

on the wall above the window frame. Install the curtain rod on the wall 8″ (20.5cm) above the mounting board, with the ends of the rod extending ½″ (1.3cm) beyond the board on both sides.

From the decorator fabric, cut two panels that are each equal to the outside window width and 88″ (224cm) long, referring to **Diagram 2.** Mark the centers at the upper and lower edges of one panel (A). Cut the other panel in half lengthwise for the side panels (B), as shown.

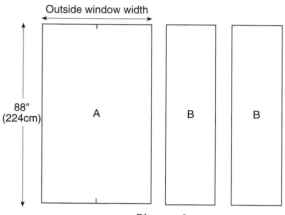

Diagram 2

From the lining fabric, cut two panels that are equal to the outside window width and 76″ (193cm) long. Mark the centers at the upper and lower edges of one panel. Cut the other panel in half lengthwise for the side panels.

SEWING DIRECTIONS

1 Assembling the shade

With right sides together, stitch the center decorator panel (A) to the two side panels (B), as shown in **Diagram 3.** Press the seams open. Repeat for the lining panels. Trim 2″ (5cm) from each side edge of the lining.

Referring to **Diagram 4,** with right sides together, pin the lining to the decorator fabric along the side edges. Place the lining 2″ (5cm) up from the lower edge of the decorator fabric. Stitch. Trim the seams. Press the seams toward the lining.

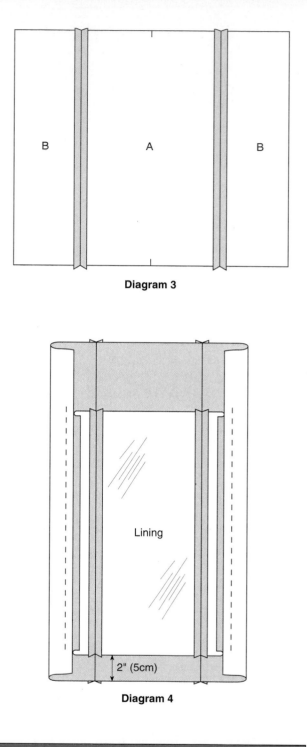

Diagram 3

Diagram 4

🧵 SEW SIMPLE

To eliminate stitching lines on the outside of the shade, use iron-on ring tape. Follow the manufacturer's directions to apply the tape.

Turn the shade right side out. Match the centers so that the decorator fabric folds back 1″ (2.5cm) on each side, as shown in **Diagram 5**. Press. Baste the layers together at the upper and lower edges of the lining.

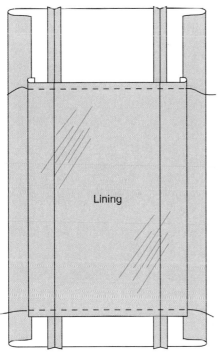

Lining

Diagram 5

2 Attaching the ring tape

On the lining side, pin one row of ring tape along each side edge. Start at the lower edge of the lining. Place each row so the first ring is 5″ (12.5cm) above the lower edge of the lining. Add four or six more rows of tape evenly spaced in between. (See the chart on page 67 for the total number of rows.) The rings should line up across the shade, as shown in **Diagram 6**.

3 Making the dowel pocket

Referring to **Diagram 7**, press under 1½″ (3.8cm) along the lower edge. Press under 1½″ (3.8cm) again. Stitch close to the second fold.

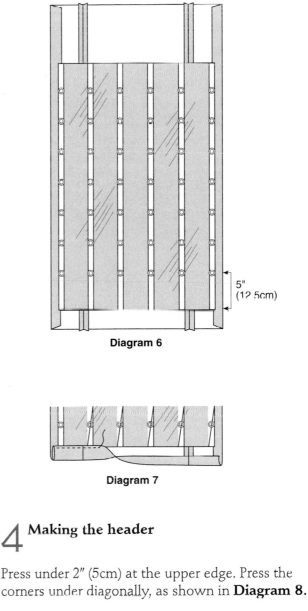

5″
(12.5cm)

Diagram 6

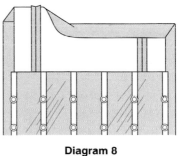

Diagram 7

4 Making the header

Press under 2″ (5cm) at the upper edge. Press the corners under diagonally, as shown in **Diagram 8**.

Diagram 8

Cut the shirring tape into two lengths equal to the width of the shade plus 2″ (5cm). Referring to

Diagram 9, pin one length 1″ (2.5cm) below the upper edge of the shade. Press the ends of the tape under 1″ (2.5cm). Use a pin to pull out the shirring cords so they are free from the folded end. Stitch the tape in place along both long edges and at the ends. Do not catch the shirring cords in the stitches. Repeat, applying the second length of shirring tape just below the first. Knot the shirring cords together in pairs at each side of the shade.

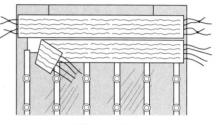

Diagram 9

Working on a flat surface, use one hand to pull one set of cords. Use the other hand to guide the gathers along the tape, as shown in **Diagram 10.** Work along the tape from one side of the shade to the center. Pull the cords from the other side to gather the remaining half of the shade. Repeat until all four pairs of cords are drawn up. The width of the gathered shade should equal the length of the mounting board. Loosely tie the cords together at the side of the shade, but do not cut the tails.

Diagram 10

5 **Rigging the shade**

Remove the mounting board from the window.

Place the shade wrong side up on a large, flat surface. Place the mounting board (on edge) on the shade, just below the shirring tape. Attach screw eyes to the underside of the board to correspond to the rows of ring tape, as shown in **Diagram 11.**

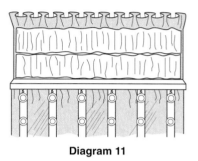

Diagram 11

Insert the dowel in the pocket at the lower edge of the shade. Distribute the fabric evenly so the rows of ring tape are parallel. Attach screw eyes to the dowel to correspond to the rows of ring tape, as shown in **Diagram 12.**

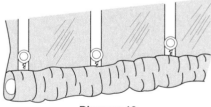

Diagram 12

Referring to **Diagram 13,** thread the nylon cord through one dowel screw eye and the four rings immediately above it. Tie the ends of the cord together. Secure the knot with a bit of glue. Thread the cord up through the remaining rings and across the top of the shade through the screw eyes to one corner. Trim the excess cord so it is even with the lower edge of the shade. Repeat for all of the rows of ring tape, running all of the cords through the screw eyes in the same direction.

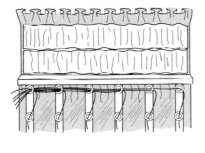

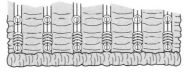

Diagram 13

Pull on the cords to draw up the shade. Loosely tie the cords together outside the last screw eye.

INSTALLATION

Reattach the mounting board at the top of the window. Have a friend help so the cords don't get tangled.

Insert the curtain hooks close to the upper edge of the shirring tape, as shown in **Diagram 14.** Attach the shade to the curtain rod.

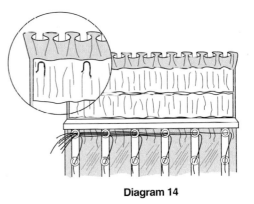

Diagram 14

Release the shade to its full length. Tie all of the ring tape cords together outside the last screw eye. Secure the knot with glue. Let the glue dry; then cut off all but one cord. Attach the weighted shade pull to the end of the cord. Attach the cleat to the side of the window frame about halfway down the window. Loop the cord around the cleat to hold the shade at the desired height.

If necessary, adjust the shirring cords at the top of the shade so the header covers the sides of the rod (called the rod returns). Retie the cords, secure the knots with glue, and cut the tails.

⊕ DESIGN PLUS

To make the mounting board as inconspicuous as possible, paint it to match the window frame.

N*ot quite a curtain . . . not quite a shade. Where privacy is a concern, this crisp, clean window treatment is the perfect choice.*

ALL BUTTONED UP

Window Size:

36″ wide × 54½″ long (91.5cm × 141cm)

SUPPLIES

- *1¾ yards (1.7m) of 45″ (115cm) wide decorator fabric, such as chintz, polished cotton, broadcloth, or taffeta*
- *1¾ yards (1.7m) of 45″ (115cm) wide contrasting decorator fabric*
- *5½ yards (5.1m) of ¾″ (2cm) wide rickrack*
- *1⅛ yards (1.1m) of 1½″ (39mm) wide grosgrain ribbon*
- *1 yard (1m) of 1½″ (3.8cm) wide sew-on loop tape*
- *1 yard (1m) of 1½″ (3.8cm) wide adhesive-backed hook tape, such as Velcro Sticky Back tape*
- *Eight 1¼″ (3.2cm) buttons*
- *Embroidery floss*
- *Dressmaker's chalk or water-soluble marking pen*

CUTTING DIRECTIONS

All measurements include ½″ (1.3cm) seam allowances.

From the decorator fabric, cut one 39″ (99cm) wide × 56½″ (144cm) long rectangle.

From the contrasting fabric, cut one 39″ (99cm) wide × 56½″ (144cm) long rectangle.

SEWING DIRECTIONS

1 Assembling the curtain

On the right side of one rectangle, use the chalk or the pen to mark a ½″ (1.3cm) seam allowance all around, as shown in **Diagram 1**.

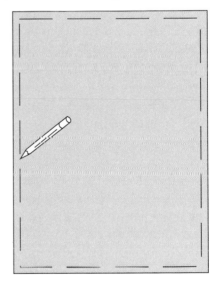

Diagram 1

Center the rickrack over the seam line. Stitch in place through the center, as shown in **Diagram 2**.

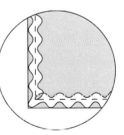

Diagram 2

🧵 SEW SIMPLE

An iron's heat can permanently set the ink of some marking pens. Test on a scrap of fabric or use a damp cloth to remove the ink marks before pressing.

With right sides together, stitch the decorator fabric to the contrasting fabric, stitching just to the left of the rickrack stitches. Leave an opening large enough for turning along the upper edge. Trim the corners, as shown in **Diagram 3.**

Diagram 3

Turn the curtain right side out and slip stitch the opening closed, following the directions on page 126 for slip stitching.

2 Finishing the curtain

Press the grosgrain ribbon in place on the back of the sew-on loop tape, turning under the ends of the ribbon. Stitch the ribbon to the outer edges of the tape, as shown in **Diagram 4.**

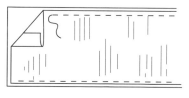

Diagram 4

Referring to **Diagram 5,** mark the ribbon for the placement of seven buttons. Place one button about 1″ (2.5cm) from each end and space the

remaining five buttons evenly in between. Sew the buttons to the ribbon with embroidery floss.

Diagram 5

Make seven vertical machine buttonholes at the top of the curtain to correspond to the button placement on the ribbon.

Make one buttonhole on the diagonal at one of the bottom corners of the curtain. The corner choice will depend on which way you want the curtain to open.

INSTALLATION

Attach the adhesive-backed hook tape at the top of the window frame. Press the button strip in place on top of it, as shown in **Diagram 6.**

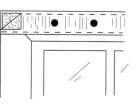

Diagram 6

Button the curtain in place at the top of the window.

Determine the best location for the pulled-back corner. Sew the remaining button at that spot, close to the side edge of the curtain, as shown in the photograph on page 72.

If desired, use double-faced carpet tape to hold the curtain close to the window at the side button area.

⊕ DESIGN PLUS

For a dressmaker's touch, use fabric-covered buttons, coordinated to the lining. To create a smooth, tight fit, wet the fabric before covering the buttons. As the fabric dries, it will shrink slightly.

CURTAINS & DRAPES

Tulips provide a breath of springtime, regardless of the season. With this simple motif, even a first-time stenciler can achieve professional results!

TULIP TIME CAFÉS

Window Size:

24" to 40" (61cm to 102cm) wide × 50" (127cm) long

SUPPLIES

- 6⅛ yards (5.7m) of 45" (115cm) wide decorator fabric, such as muslin, chintz, or broadcloth
- 2 café curtain rods

STENCILING (optional)

- *Oiled stencil paper or stencil acetate*
- *Graphite paper for transferring the design*
- *Craft knife*
- *Three ½" (1.3cm) flat stencil brushes*
- *3 colors of stencil paint cream, such as Stencil Magic*
- *Soap and water or turpentine to clean brushes, as directed by the paint manufacturer*
- *Fixative spray, such as Krylon*

CUTTING DIRECTIONS

All measurements include ½" (1.3cm) seam allowances.

From the decorator fabric, cut the following pieces, as shown in **Diagram 1:**

- *Two 45" × 56" (115cm × 143cm) curtains (A)*
- *One 22" × 84" (56cm × 214cm) valance (B)*

Trim off the selvage edges.

From the remaining decorator fabric, cut twenty-six 4½" × 7" (11.5cm × 18cm) tabs.

SEWING DIRECTIONS

1 Making the tabs

With right sides together, fold each tab in half lengthwise. Stitch the long edges together, as shown in **Diagram 2.**

Diagram 2

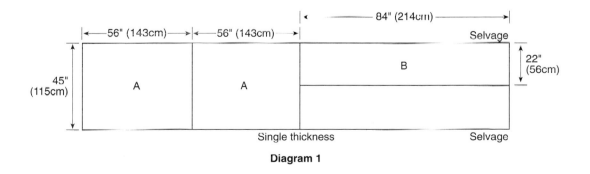

Diagram 1

These light, bright curtains combine traditional styling with up-to-the-minute hardware.

SHEER BEAUTY

Window Size:

30" to 40" (76cm to 102cm) wide

SUPPLIES

- *60" or 120" (153cm or 305cm) wide sheer or lace decorator fabric**
- *2" (5cm) wide flat lace edging**
- *1 standard curtain rod*
- *2 decorative push pin holdbacks*

*See the "Cutting Directions" for additional information.

CUTTING DIRECTIONS

Install the rod at the top of the window frame. Measure the window from the top of the rod to the desired finished length of the curtain. Consult the chart below to determine how much fabric and edging to purchase.

For 60" (153cm) wide fabric, fold the fabric in half crosswise and and cut along the fold. Cut two panels to correspond to your window length, as shown in **Diagram 1**.

For 120" (305cm) wide fabric, fold the fabric in half lengthwise with selvage edges matching. Cut along the fold to form two 60" (153cm) wide pieces. Cut two panels to correspond to your window length.

FINISHED LENGTH	60" (153CM) WIDE FABRIC	120" (305CM) WIDE FABRIC	2" (5CM) WIDE EDGING
45" (115cm)	3 yards (2.8m)	1½ yards (1.4m)	6½ yards (5.9m)
54" (138cm)	3½ yards (3.3m)	1¾ yards (1.7m)	7 yards (6.4m)
63" (160cm)	3⅞ yards (3.6m)	2 yards (1.9m)	7½ yards (6.9m)
72" (183cm)	4½ yards (4.2m)	2¼ yards (2.1m)	8 yards (7.3m)
84" (214cm)	5⅛ yards (4.7m)	2⅝ yards (2.5m)	8⅝ yards (7.9m)
90" (229cm)	5½ yards (5.1m)	2¾ yards (2.6m)	9 yards (8.2m)
95" (242cm)	5¾ yards (5.3m)	2⅞ yards (2.7m)	9¼ yards (8.5m)

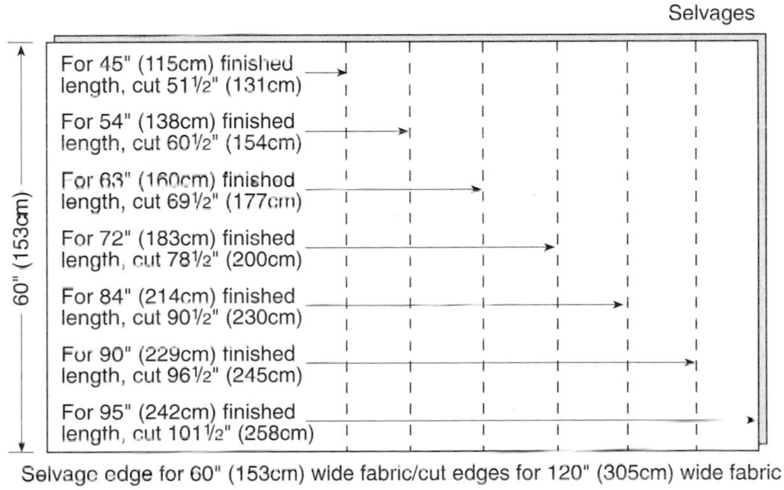

Selvages

60" (153cm)

For 45" (115cm) finished length, cut 51½" (131cm)

For 54" (138cm) finished length, cut 60½" (154cm)

For 63" (160cm) finished length, cut 69½" (177cm)

For 72" (183cm) finished length, cut 78½" (200cm)

For 84" (214cm) finished length, cut 90½" (230cm)

For 90" (229cm) finished length, cut 96½" (245cm)

For 95" (242cm) finished length, cut 101½" (258cm)

Selvage edge for 60" (153cm) wide fabric/cut edges for 120" (305cm) wide fabric

Diagram 1

SEWING DIRECTIONS

1 Applying the lace edging

Pin the wrong side of edging to right side of fabric along one long edge of a panel. Keep the scalloped border even with the cut edge of the panel. Pin the edging all the way to the corner. Stitch close to the straight border of the edging. Stop stitching approximately 5″ (12.5cm) from the corner, as shown in **Diagram 2.**

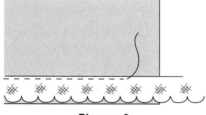

Diagram 2

Fold the edging back on itself. Then refold the edging, keeping the scalloped border aligned with the panel edge, as shown in **Diagram 3.** A dart will form at the corner. Press the corner. Unpin the edging. Stitch the dart, as shown in **Diagram 4.** Trim the dart close to the stitching.

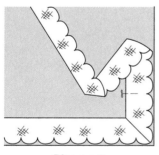

Diagram 3

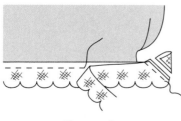

Diagram 4

🧵 SEW SIMPLE

Examine your lace fabric carefully to see whether it has a one-directional motif and/or a right and wrong side. If so, mark the top of each panel, on the right side of the fabric, with a dot of masking tape before applying the edging.

Repin the edging. Finish stitching along the straight border, as shown in **Diagram 5.**

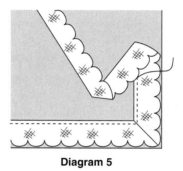

Diagram 5

Referring to **Diagram 6,** press the hem allowance away from the edging. On the right side of the panel, stitch close to the straight border of the edging through all thicknesses. Trim the hem allowance close to the stitching.

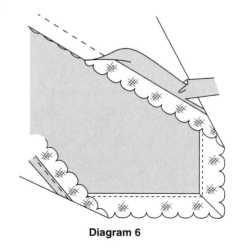

Diagram 6

Apply lace edging to the other panel in the same manner, making a mirror image of the first panel.

2 Finishing the panels

Press under 1" (2.5cm) on the untrimmed long edges of both panels. Tuck each raw edge under to meet the crease. Press. Stitch close to the second fold, as shown in **Diagram 7**.

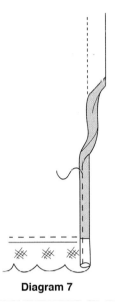

Diagram 7

Referring to **Diagram 8,** press under 4½" (11.5cm) along the upper edges of both panels. Press under ½" (1.3cm) along each raw edge. Stitch close to the second fold. Stitch again 2" (5cm) below the upper edge, creating a 2" (5cm) header and a 2" (5cm) rod pocket.

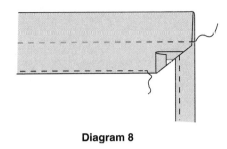

Diagram 8

INSTALLATION

Hang the curtains on the rod with the lace edging at the center. Arrange each panel by forming a soft drape in the center. Use the push pin holdbacks to secure the panels at the sides of the window frame, as shown in the photograph on page 82.

Bountiful bows set the tone for these feminine—yet
formal—drapes that add richness
and drama to any room.

A BEVY OF BOWS

Window Size:

Windows or French doors that measure 36″ to 48″ (91.5cm to 122cm) wide and 12″ (30.5cm) down from an 8′ (244cm) high ceiling. The drapes puddle approximately 6″ to 8″ (15cm to 20.5cm) on the floor.

Note: The doors should open out, away from the drapes.

SUPPLIES

- *7⅜ yards (6.8m) of 54″ to 60″ (138cm to 153cm) wide decorator fabric, such as moiré, taffeta, antique satin, chintz, or polished cotton*
- *3 yards (2.8m) of standard pleater tape with a 2:1 pleating ratio (check the manufacturer's information)*
- *1 decorative pole rod and 7 rings for pleater hooks*
- *8 locking pleater hooks for decorative pole rod*
- *2 decorative push pin holdbacks*
- *Air-soluble marking pen*

⊕ DESIGN PLUS

For a tailored look, minus the bows, purchase 5⅜ yards (5m) of fabric. After the drapes are installed, hand sew the center pleats together so they fall smoothly from the center ring.

CUTTING DIRECTIONS

All measurements include ½″ (1.3cm) seam allowances.

From the decorator fabric, cut the following:

- *2 drapery panels, each 52½″ × 95″ (133cm × 242cm)*
- *14 bow sections, each 5″ × 44″ (12.5cm × 112cm)*

Cut the pleater tape into two sections, with 32 spaces in each section. Each section should begin and end with a full space. Trim the beginning and ending spaces to 1″ (2.5cm), as shown in **Diagram 1.**

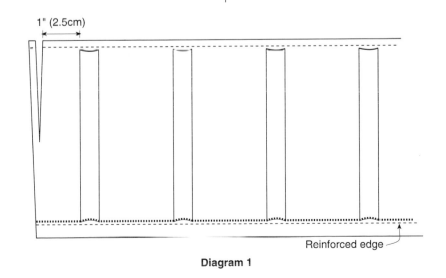

Diagram 1

SEWING DIRECTIONS

1 Hemming the drapes

Press under 1" (2.5cm) on the side edges of each panel, then 1" (2.5cm) again. Stitch close to the first fold, as shown in **Diagram 2.**

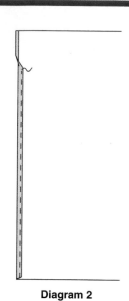

Diagram 2

Press the lower edge of each panel up 4½" (11.5cm). Press the raw edge under ½" (1.3cm). Stitch close to the inner fold, as shown in **Diagram 3.**

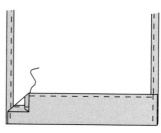

Diagram 3

2 Making the pleats

Working on the right side of one panel, measure down ½" (1.3cm) from the upper edge and draw a placement line across the top of the panel with the marking pen, as shown in **Diagram 4.**

Examine the pleater tape to identify the reinforced pocket edge. Pin the pleater tape, pocket side up, to the panel, matching the edge of the pleater tape that is not reinforced to the placement line. Turn the side edges of the tape under ½" (1.3cm). Stitch the pleater tape to the panel ¼" (6mm) above the placement line, as shown in **Diagram 5.**

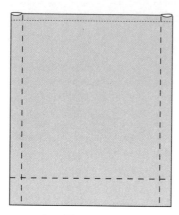

Diagram 4

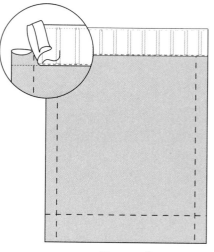

Diagram 5

Fold the pleater tape down onto the wrong side of the panel; press. Stitch the tape to the panel along the side edges and the remaining long edge, as shown in **Diagram 6.**

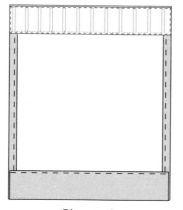

Diagram 6

Referring to **Diagram 7,** use a pleater hook and the first four pockets to make a pleat at one end of the pleater tape. Count off six spaces on the pleater tape (approximately 9″ [23cm]) and make the second pleat. Count off six more spaces and make the third pleat. Use the last four pockets on the tape to make the fourth pleat.

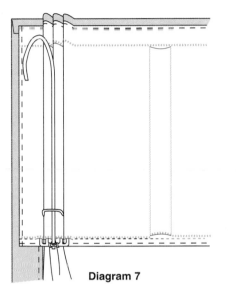

Diagram 7

Repeat, making the pleats on the other panel.

3 Making the bows

Referring to **Diagram 8,** pin two bow sections with right sides together. Working on one long edge, measure in 1½″ (3.8cm) from one short edge and mark. Draw a diagonal line from the mark to the corresponding corner on the opposite long edge. Repeat for the other end. Trim along both lines.

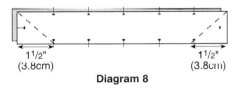

1½″
(3.8cm)   1½″
                        (3.8cm)
Diagram 8

Stitch around the raw edges, leaving a 6″ (15cm) opening at the center of the longest edge for turning, as shown in **Diagram 9.** Trim the seam allowances and corners. Turn the strip right side out and press it flat, tucking the raw edges in evenly along the opening. Slip stitch the opening closed, following the directions on page 126 for slip stitching.

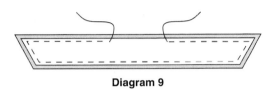

Diagram 9

Tie the strip in a bow, following the directions on page 128 for tying a bow.

Repeat, making six more bows.

🧵 SEW SIMPLE

Instead of slip stitching the strip opening closed, tuck a piece of fusible web inside the pressed strip, between the seam allowances. Fuse as directed by the fusible web manufacturer.

INSTALLATION

Install the pole rod and rings on the frame above the window or doors. Hang the drapes on the rings, using the center ring for the two center pleats, as shown in the photograph on page 86. Pin or hand sew the bows in place at the bottom of the pleats, aligning the bows with the rings. Use the push pin holdbacks to secure the drapes at the sides of the frame. Gently shape the dips across the top of the drapes between the pleats.

Our self-lined construction technique means easy sewing, a full-bodied appearance, and high eye appeal from both inside and outside the house.

TAILORED TABS

Window Size:

24" to 40" (61cm to 102cm) wide × 50" (127cm) long

SUPPLIES

- *7½ yards (6.9m) of 45" (115cm) wide decorator fabric, such as chintz, polished cotton, sateen, or broadcloth*
- *1 café curtain rod*

CUTTING DIRECTIONS

All measurements include ½" (1.3cm) seam allowances.

From the decorator fabric, cut the following pieces:

- *Four 45" × 62" (115cm × 158cm) panels*
- *Fourteen 4½" × 7" (11.5cm × 18cm) tabs*

SEW SIMPLE

If your fabric has a one-way motif, mark the top of each panel before assembling the curtains. This will ensure that the motif runs in the same direction on both sides of the curtain.

SEWING DIRECTIONS

1 Making the tabs

With right sides together, fold each tab in half lengthwise. Stitch the long edges together, as shown in **Diagram 1**.

Diagram 1

Turn each tab right side out. Press. Fold in half, as shown in **Diagram 2**, and machine baste the raw edges together.

Diagram 2

2 Assembling the curtains

On the right side of one panel and along the upper edge, pin one tab ¾" (2cm) in from each side edge and space five tabs evenly in between. The raw edges of the tabs should be even with the upper edge of the panel. Machine baste the tabs in place, as shown in **Diagram 3**.

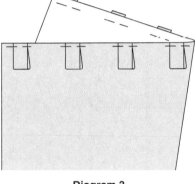

Diagram 3

With right sides together, pin two panels together. Stitch. Leave an opening along one side edge large enough for turning. Trim the corners, as shown in **Diagram 4**.

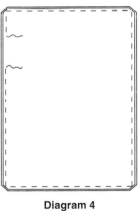

Diagram 4

Assemble the other curtain in the same manner.

Turn each curtain right side out. Press. Slip stitch the openings closed, following the directions on page 126 for slip stitching.

INSTALLATION

Install the café rod at the top of the window. Hang the curtains, as shown in the photograph.

It takes less than an hour to make this thoroughly modern window treatment with neoclassical roots.

ARTFUL DRAPE

Window Size:

30" to 40" (76cm to 102cm) wide

SUPPLIES

- *60" (153cm) wide sheer or lace fabric**
- *4 decorative push pin holdbacks*

*See the "Cutting Directions" for additional information.

CUTTING DIRECTIONS

Referring to **Diagram 1,** measure the window from the top of the window frame to the floor. Consult the chart below to determine how much fabric to purchase.

From the fabric, cut one panel, as shown in **Diagram 2.**

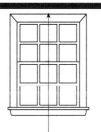

Diagram 1

WINDOW TO FLOOR	AMOUNT OF 60" (153CM) WIDE FABRIC
84" (214cm)	2½ yards (2.3m)
90" (229cm)	2⅝ yards (2.5m)
95" (242cm)	2¾ yards (2.6m)

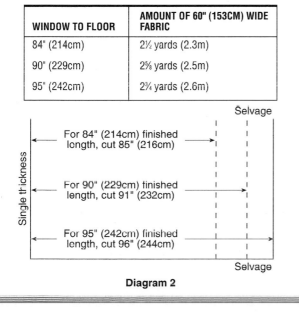

Diagram 2

SEWING DIRECTIONS

Trim off the selvage edges on the long edges of the panel.

Press under ½" (1.3cm) on all edges of the panel.

Referring to **Diagram 3,** open out the corners. Turn under each corner diagonally where the pressed lines intersect. Trim the corner hem allowance to ¼" (6mm).

Diagram 3

Tuck the raw edges under to meet the crease along all four sides of the panel. Stitch close to the second fold, as shown in **Diagram 4.**

Diagram 4

INSTALLATION

Fold the curtain in half lengthwise. Pin mark the center fold at the upper edge.

Measure and mark the center of the window at the top of the window frame. Open out the curtain. Match the center mark on the curtain to the center mark on the window and attach the curtain with a decorative push pin holdback. Use push pin holdbacks to attach the upper corners of the curtain to the corresponding corners of the window frame.

Arrange the curtain to form a soft drape on one side, as shown in the photograph. Use the remaining holdback to hold the drape in place in the desired position on the side of the window frame.

🧵 SEW SIMPLE

If you have access to an overlock machine, use the narrow rolled hem stitch to fast-finish the edges.

Bring the outdoors indoors with an opulent cornice fashioned from dried flowers and installed atop a pair of easy, gathered curtains.

FLORAL FANTASY

Window Size:

36″ wide × 54″ long (91.5cm × 138cm). The length of the curtain panels is based on a room with 8′ (244cm) ceilings and windows that are approximately 12″ (30.5cm) from the ceiling.

SUPPLIES

- *6 yards (5.5m) of 45″ to 60″ (115cm to 153cm) wide decorator fabric, such as chintz, antique satin, moiré, batiste, or voile*

- *1 standard double curtain rod*

CORNICE (optional)

- *One 36″ (91.5cm) long piece of wood (a 1″ × 3″ [2.5cm × 7.5cm] furring strip is perfect)*

- *4 large drapery hooks and 8 screws*

- *Floral materials to coordinate with your fabric (here, we used 6 medium bags of natural Spanish moss, 1 medium bunch of preserved baby eucalyptus, 3 medium bunches of dried German statice, 1 small bunch of caspia, 1 small bunch of dried statice, and 3 small bunches of mini-baby's-breath)*

- *8 yards (7.4m) of ⅞″ (23mm) wide moiré ribbon*

- *28-gauge wire*

- *Hot-glue gun and glue sticks*

CUTTING DIRECTIONS

From the decorator fabric, cut two panels, each 3 yards (2.8m) long. Trim off the selvage edges.

SEWING DIRECTIONS

1 Hemming the sides

Press under 1″ (2.5cm) on each side of each panel, then 1″ (2.5cm) again. Stitch close to the first fold, as shown in **Diagram 1.**

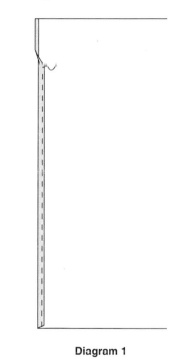

Diagram 1

🧵 SEW SIMPLE

Drapery weights will help keep your curtains hanging nice and straight. After pressing up the bottom hem, hand sew a drapery weight to the side hem allowance at each bottom corner; then stitch the hem in place.

2 Making the rod pockets

Press under ½" (1.3cm) along the upper edge of each panel. Press under again, 1½" (3.8cm). Stitch close to the first fold, as shown in **Diagram 2.**

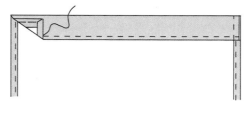

Diagram 2

3 Finishing the panels

Install the curtain rod at the top of the window frame. Measure from the top of the rod to the floor. Measure and cut each panel to equal this measurement plus 4½" (11.5cm).

Press the lower edge of each panel up 4½" (11.5cm). Press the raw edge under ½" (1.3cm). Stitch close to the inner fold, as shown in **Diagram 3.**

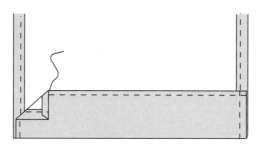

Diagram 3

✦ DESIGN PLUS

For a truly luxurious look, add 6" (15cm) to the length of each panel so that the curtains will puddle on the floor.

CORNICE DIRECTIONS

1 Preparing the furring strip

Attach the hooks to the back of the furring strip, placing one at each end and spacing the other two evenly in between. Screw them into the wood, securing them well.

2 Applying the dried flowers

Pull the moss apart and glue it to the front of the wood. Press it down, being careful not to burn yourself.

Cut the eucalyptus into 4" to 5" (10cm to 12.5cm) pieces and glue them all around the cornice.

Cut the statice into 5" to 6" (12.5cm to 15cm) pieces. Glue these pieces onto the cornice, filling in between the eucalyptus.

Cut the caspia into 5" (12.5cm) pieces. Stagger and glue these amid the statice.

Cut the stems off the baby's-breath, leaving the heads in groups of four. Glue them around the cornice.

3 Making the bows

Cut the ribbon in half to make two florist bows.

For each bow, start with a 3" to 3½" (7.5cm to 9cm) loop, leaving an 18" (45.5cm) tail. Continue looping the ribbon back and forth, as shown in **Diagram 4,** twisting the ribbon between each loop and making 13 more 3" to 3½" (7.5cm to 9cm) loops. Finish the bow with one 12" (30.5cm) loop. Wrap the wire tightly at the center of the loops (see **Diagram 5**). Cut the 12" (30.5cm) loop in half to form two tails; notch the end of each tail.

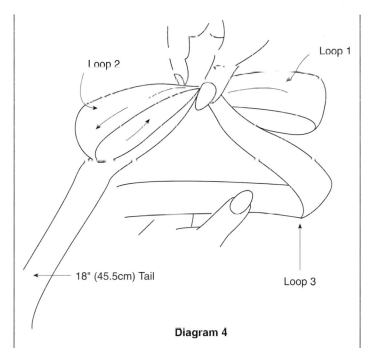

Loop 2

Loop 1

Loop 3

← —— 18" (45.5cm) Tail

Diagram 4

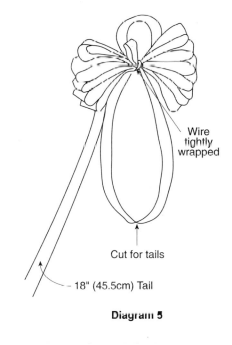

Wire
tightly
wrapped

Cut for tails

- 18" (45.5cm) Tail

Diagram 5

Separate the loops by placing your finger inside the first loop and twisting in one direction. Twist the loop below it in the opposite direction. Continue doing this for all of the loops.

Glue one bow at each end of the cornice. Let the short tails hang down. Twist and tuck the longer tails through the other flowers and have them meet in the middle. Use dabs of glue to hold the tails in place.

Fill in any bare spots with additional floral materials, gluing them evenly throughout the cornice.

INSTALLATION

Hang the curtain panels on the inner curtain rod.

Hang the cornice on the outer curtain rod.

Recall the romance of bygone eras with delicate lace curtains and matching festoon.

VICTORIAN DELIGHT

Window Size:

36" (91.5cm) wide × 40" to 60" (102cm to 153cm) long. The length of the curtain panels is based on a room with 8' (244cm) ceilings and windows that are approximately 12" (30.5cm) from the ceiling. The bottoms of the curtains puddle approximately 3" (7.5cm) on the floor.

SUPPLIES

- *8¾ yards (8.1m) of 45" (115cm) wide lace fabric*
- *2¼ yards (2.1m) of 45" (115cm) wide tulle*
- *1½ yards (1.4m) of 3½" (9cm) wide pregathered lace trim*
- *1½ yards (1.4m) of 45" (115cm) wide nonwoven pattern-duplicating material*
- *2 yards (1.9m) of nylon cable cord*
- *2 cup hooks*
- *Two 1" (2.5cm) diameter plastic rings*
- *One 2½" (6.3cm) wide continental rod*
- *1 double curtain rod*
- *Masking tape*

CUTTING DIRECTIONS

All measurements include ½" (1.3cm) seam allowances.

From the lace fabric, cut two curtain panels, each 45" (115cm) wide × 108" (275cm) long.

Using the pattern-duplicating material, create the valance pattern, as shown in **Diagram 1**.

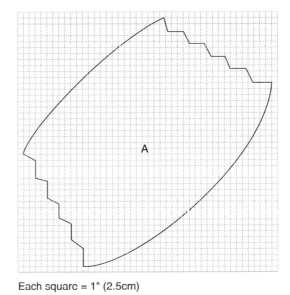

Each square = 1" (2.5cm)

Diagram 1

From the remaining lace fabric, cut the following pieces, using the patterns shown in **Diagram 2** and in **Diagram 3** on page 100:

- *1 festoon (A)*
- *One 4½" × 37" (11.5cm × 94cm) casing (B)*
- *Two 7½" × 45" (19cm × 115cm) rod covers (C)*
- *Four 5" × 45" (12.5cm × 115cm) bows with slanted ends (D)*
- *Two 4" × 5" (10cm × 12.5cm) knots (E)*

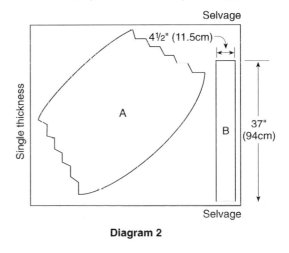

Diagram 2

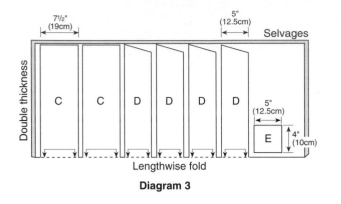

Diagram 3

From the tulle fabric, cut the following pieces, using the patterns shown in **Diagram 4:**

- *1 festoon lining (A)*
- *Two 5″ × 45″ (12.5cm × 115cm) bow interfacings (D)*

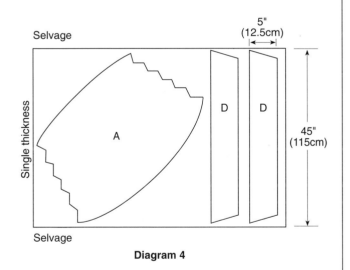

Diagram 4

SEWING DIRECTIONS

1 Making the curtains

Press the selvage edges of each curtain panel under 1″ (2.5cm). Tuck each selvage edge under to meet the crease. Press. Stitch close to the second fold, as shown in **Diagram 5.**

Diagram 5

Referring to **Diagram 6,** press under ½″ (1.3cm) along the upper edge of the panel. Press under again 3″ (7.5cm). Stitch close to the first fold. Stitch again 1″ (2.5cm) from the upper edge to form a 2″ (5cm) rod pocket and a 1″ (2.5cm) header.

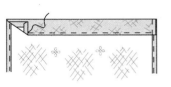

Diagram 6

Referring to **Diagram 7,** press under 4½″ (11.5cm) along the lower edge. Tuck the raw edge under ½″ (1.3cm). Press. Stitch close to the second fold.

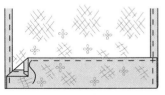

Diagram 7

🧵 SEW SIMPLE

Examine your lace carefully. If it has an attractively finished selvage edge, there's no need to hem the sides of these panels.

2 Assembling the festoon

With right sides together, stitch the lace festoon to the tulle festoon along the lower edge, as shown in **Diagram 8.** Trim the seam allowances.

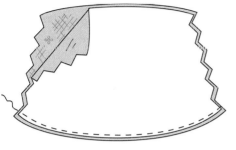

Diagram 8

Turn the festoon right side out and press the lower edge. Baste the layers together along the upper and side edges, as shown in **Diagram 9.**

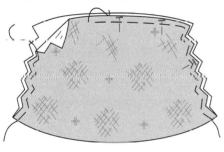

Diagram 9

To shape the festoon, start on one side at the lower edge. Referring to **Diagram 10,** make a soft fold along the edge at the first indentation. Bring the fold up to the next indentation and pin in place at the side of the festoon. Repeat, making five pleats on each side of the festoon.

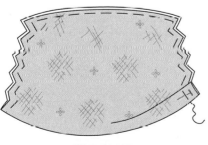

Diagram 10

To check the shape and width of the festoon, pin it to the edge of an ironing board, as shown in **Diagram 11.** Adjust the pleats, as necessary, so that the folds are even and the festoon measures approximately 35½″ (90cm) across the top.

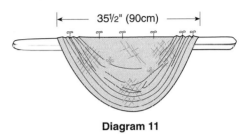

Diagram 11

Remove the festoon from the ironing board. Baste the layers together across the top, as shown in **Diagram 12.**

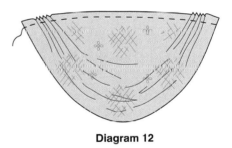

Diagram 12

3 Making the festoon casing

Press under ¼″ (6mm) along the ends of the casing. Press under again ½″ (1.3cm). Stitch close to the first fold, as shown in **Diagram 13.** Fold the casing in half lengthwise, with wrong sides together, and press.

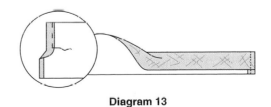

Diagram 13

With right sides together, pin the casing to the festoon, as shown in **Diagram 14.** If necessary, ease the festoon to fit. Stitch. Press the casing up, away from the festoon.

Diagram 14

4 Applying the festoon trim

Pin the lace trim in place along the lower edge of the festoon, lapping the edge of the festoon over the upper edge of the trim and turning the ends of the trim under. Topstitch the trim along the seam, as shown in **Diagram 15.**

Diagram 15

5 Making the rod cover

With right sides together, stitch the two rod cover pieces together to form the center front seam, as shown in **Diagram 16.** Press the seam to one side. Press under ¼" (6mm) along the ends of the cover. Press under again ½" (1.3cm). Stitch close to the first fold.

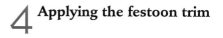

Diagram 16

Fold the cover in half lengthwise, with right sides together, and stitch the long seam, as shown in **Diagram 17.** Trim the seam. Turn the cover right side out and press.

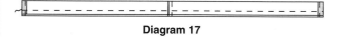

Diagram 17

6 Making the bows

Baste the tulle bow interfacing pieces to the wrong side of two bow pieces.

With right sides together, stitch one interfaced bow piece to one plain bow piece, leaving an opening in the center large enough for turning. Trim the corners, as shown in **Diagram 18.** Turn the bow right side out and slip stitch the opening closed, following the directions on page 126 for slip stitching.

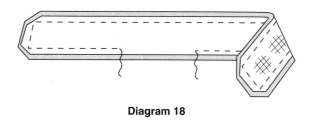

Diagram 18

Fold the bow in half crosswise. Measure 10" (25.5cm) from the fold and mark. Stitch across the bow at the marking. Refold the bow so that the center fold meets the stitching line, as shown in **Diagram 19.**

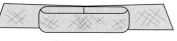

Diagram 19

Fold one knot piece in half lengthwise, with right sides together, and stitch the seam, as shown in **Diagram 20.** Turn the knot piece right side out and press.

Diagram 20

Referring to **Diagram 21,** pleat the bow at the center to form two horizontal folds. Wrap the knot around the center of the bow and hand sew the edges together on the back of the bow.

Repeat to make the second bow.

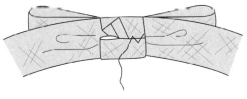

Diagram 21

INSTALLATION

Install the rods at the top of the window frame so that the double rod is behind the continental rod. Referring to **Diagram 22,** hang the festoon on the back double rod. Hang the curtain panels on the front double rod. Drape the festoon over the curtains and arrange the folds. Slip the rod cover over the continental rod. Pin the bows in place at the corners of the continental rod.

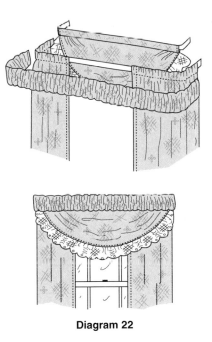

Diagram 22

Determine the location of the side poufs by tying a piece of cable cord around each curtain. Adjust the poufs to create a pleasing proportion, allowing some of the curtain to puddle on the floor.

Temporarily secure the cords to the window frame with a bit of masking tape. Attach the cup hooks to the window frame at the desired locations. Tie the curtain rings onto the cords. Attach the curtain rings to the cup hooks. Conceal the cord tails behind the curtain panels. To keep the poufs from sagging, stuff them with the leftover tulle.

✦ DESIGN PLUS

For a smoother pouf, loosely accordion pleat the panel; then tie the pouf to the wall.

*S*ewing is a snap with ribbon tabs and tiebacks.
Ribbon is a great time-saver . . . . and it's a terrific
attention getter, too!

Window Size:

24" to 40" (61cm to 102cm) wide × 50" (127cm) long

SUPPLIES

- *4⅝ yards (4.3m) of 45" (115cm) wide decorator fabric, such as chintz, polished cotton, sateen, or broadcloth*
- *4⅝ yards (4.3m) of 45" wide lining fabric, such as polished cotton or broadcloth*
- *4 yards (3.7m) of 2¼" (56mm) wide grosgrain ribbon*
- *2 small plastic rings*
- *2 cup hooks or tieback wedges*
- *1 café curtain rod*

CUTTING DIRECTIONS

All measurements include ½" (1.3cm) seam allowances.

From the decorator fabric, cut two 45" × 83" (115cm × 211cm) panel pieces. Mark the upper edge of each panel ¾" (2cm) in from each side (selvage) edge, as shown in **Diagram 1**.

From the lining fabric, cut two 45" × 83" (115cm × 211cm) lining panel pieces.

From the ribbon, cut twelve 7" (18cm) tab pieces. Cut the remaining ribbon in half for the two tieback pieces.

SEWING DIRECTIONS

1 Assembling the curtains

Fold each ribbon tab piece in half crosswise and pin, as shown in **Diagram 2**.

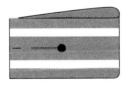

Diagram 2

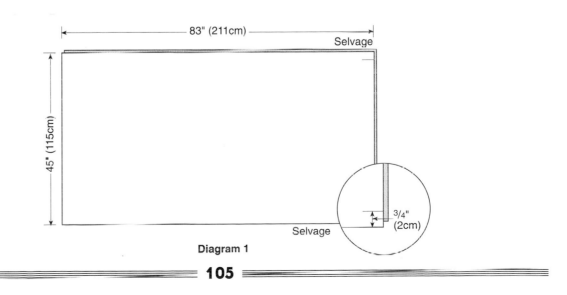

Diagram 1

Soft, Victorian-inspired swags sweep across the top of coordinating curtains.

SWOOP-TOP CURTAINS

Window Size:

36" to 40" (91.5cm to 102cm) wide × 50" (127cm) long and 12" (30.5cm) down from an 8' (244cm) high ceiling

SUPPLIES

- *5¾ yards (5.3m) of 45" (115cm) wide decorator fabric, such as polished cotton, chintz, moiré, or taffeta*
- *2¼ yards (2.1m) of 45" (115cm) wide contrasting decorator fabric, such as polished cotton, chintz, moiré, or taffeta*
- *1 standard curtain rod*

CUTTING DIRECTIONS

All measurements include ½" (1.3cm) seam allowances.

From the decorator fabric, cut two curtain panels, each 101" (257cm) long × the full width of the fabric.

From the contrasting decorator fabric, cut the following pieces, using the patterns shown in **Diagram 1:**

- *Two 29" × 45" (73.5cm × 115cm) swags*
- *Four 5" (12.5cm) wide ruffle strips*

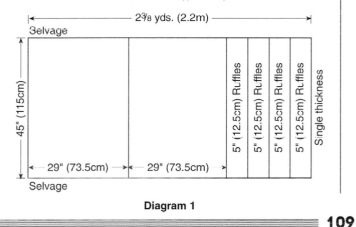

Diagram 1

Pin the two swag pieces with right sides together and cut edges matching. On one long edge, measure in 10" (25.5cm) and mark. Draw a diagonal line, as shown in **Diagram 2.** Cut off the triangle.

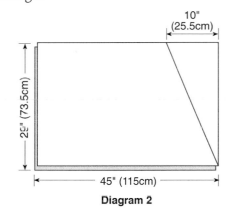

Diagram 2

SEWING DIRECTIONS

1 Hemming the curtains

Press under 1" (2.5cm) on each side edge of each panel, then 1" (2.5cm) again. Stitch close to the first fold, as shown in **Diagram 3.**

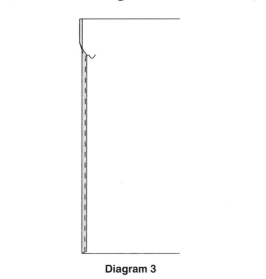

Diagram 3

Press the lower edge of each panel up 4½″ (11.5cm). Press the raw edge under ½″ (1.3cm). Stitch close to the second fold, as shown in **Diagram 4.**

Diagram 4

2 Making the curtain headers and rod pockets

Referring to **Diagram 5,** press under 4½″ (11.5cm) along the upper edge of each panel. Press under ½″ (1.3cm) along the raw edge. Stitch close to the second fold. Stitch again 2″ (5cm) below the upper edge, creating a 2″ (5cm) header and a 2″ (5cm) rod pocket.

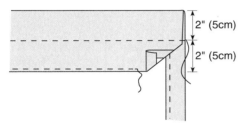

2″ (5cm)
2″ (5cm)

Diagram 5

3 Hemming the swags

Press under ½″ (1.3cm) on each long edge of the swags, then ½″ (1.3cm) again. Stitch close to the first fold, as shown in **Diagram 6.**

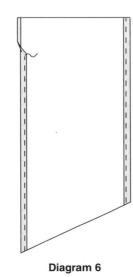

Diagram 6

4 Making the swag headers and rod pockets

Referring to **Diagram 7,** press under 4½″ (11.5cm) along the upper edge of each panel. Press under ½″ (1.3cm) along the raw edge. Stitch close to the second fold. Stitch again 2″ (5cm) below the upper edge, creating a 2″ (5cm) header and a 2″ (5cm) rod pocket.

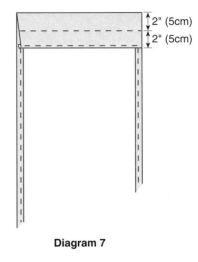

2″ (5cm)
2″ (5cm)

Diagram 7

5 Making the rod casings

Press under ½″ (1.3cm) along the diagonal edge of each panel, then 2″ (5cm) again. Stitch close to the first fold, creating a 2″ (5cm) rod casing, as shown in **Diagram 8.**

2″ (5cm)

Diagram 8

🧵 SEW SIMPLE

Machine baste with water-soluble thread in the top of the machine and all-purpose thread in the bobbin. Once the ruffle is gathered and attached, a light touch with a steam iron will dissolve the top thread. The bobbin thread will fall away.

6 Hemming the ruffles

Stitch two ruffle sections together to make one long ruffle. Repeat, making a second long ruffle.

Press under ½" (1.3cm) on one long edge of one ruffle. Press under ½" (1.3cm) again. Stitch close to the first fold, as shown in **Diagram 9.** Repeat, hemming all four edges of both ruffles.

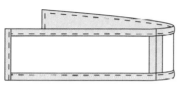

Diagram 9

7 Attaching the ruffles

Referring to **Diagram 10,** machine baste along one long edge of each ruffle, using two rows of stitches. Place the rows 1" (2.5cm) and ½" (1.3cm) from the edge. Divide and mark the edge into eight equal parts.

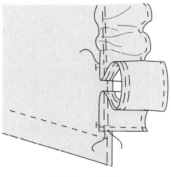

Diagram 10

Divide and mark the long edge of each swag, between the rod pocket and casing, into eight equal parts.

Working on the right side of each swag, lap the ruffles over the long side edges between the rod pocket and the casing. Center the machine basting over the hem allowance. Match and pin at the markings.

Draw up the basting stitches, gathering the ruffle until it fits. Adjust the gathers; then topstitch the

ruffle in place between the two rows of basting stitches, as shown in **Diagram 11.** Remove the basting stitches.

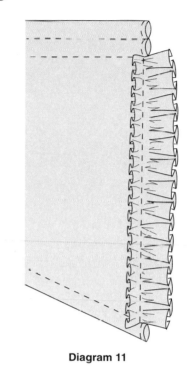

Diagram 11

INSTALLATION

Install the rod at the top of the window. Hang the swags so they are at the center of the rod. Hang one curtain panel on each side of the swags, as shown in the photograph on page 108. Pull each swag up and thread the curtain rod through the lower casing. Adjust the swag, squeezing the lower casing to fit on the rod return. Distribute the remaining fullness evenly across the window.

⊕ DESIGN PLUS

For a lighthearted, delicate interpretation of this window treatment, use a semi-transparent fabric, such as voile, lace, or dotted swiss. Match the swags to the curtains. Make two fabric bows, following the directions on page 128 for tying a bow. After the window treatment is installed, hand sew the bows to the swags at each outside corner.

Match the fabric to your needs! Choose opaque fabrics for full privacy or sheers for let-in-the-light loveliness.

ROMANTIC PANELS

Door Size:

Single or double doors with glass panels that measure approximately 25″ × 63″ (63.5cm × 160cm)

SUPPLIES

- *45″ (115cm) wide decorator fabric, such as chintz, broadcloth, polished cotton, voile, lace, or dotted swiss**
- *2 sash rods or spring tension rods per door*

*See the "Cutting Directions" for additional information.

CUTTING DIRECTIONS

All measurements include ½″ (1.3cm) seam allowances.

Install the rods at the top and bottom of the glass panel(s). Measure from the upper edge of the top rod to the lower edge of the bottom rod, as shown in **Diagram 1**. To determine the cutting length for each panel, add 18″ (45.5cm) to this measurement.

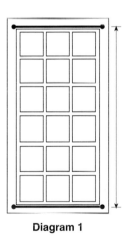

Diagram 1

To determine how many yards (meters) of fabric to purchase for each glass panel, divide the cutting length by 36″ (91.5cm). For the ruffles and tieback, add 1⅝ yards (1.5m) to this amount. For double doors, as shown in the photograph, purchase twice this amount of fabric.

For each door, cut one panel, seven 5″ × 45″ (12.5cm × 115cm) ruffle sections, and two 10″ × 45″ (25.5cm × 115cm) tieback sections from the decorator fabric, as shown in **Diagram 2**.

Fold the panel in half lengthwise. At the upper edge of the panel, measure down 2″ (5cm) along the fold and mark, as shown in **Diagram 3**. Draw a diagonal line from this mark to the upper outside corner of the panel. Curve the line slightly to eliminate the point at the fold. Trim along this line. Repeat for the lower edge of the panel.

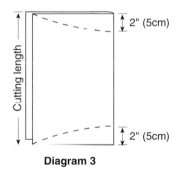

Diagram 3

For double doors, repeat for a second panel.

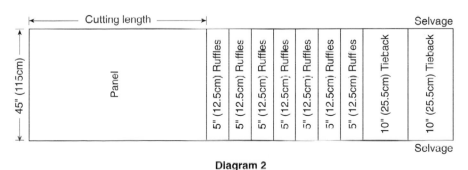

Diagram 2

SEWING DIRECTIONS

For double doors, follow these directions for each panel.

1 Hemming the panel

Press under ½″ (1.3cm) on each long edge of the panel, then ½″ (1.3cm) again. Stitch close to the first fold, as shown in **Diagram 4.**

Diagram 4

2 Making the headers and rod pockets

Referring to **Diagram 5,** press under 4½″ (11.5cm) along the upper edge of the panel. Press under ½″ (1.3cm) along the raw edge. Stitch close to the second fold. Stitch again 2″ (5cm) below the upper edge, creating a 2″ (5cm) header and a 2″ (5cm) rod pocket.

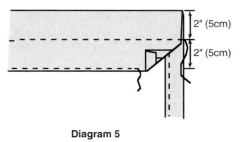

2″ (5cm)

2″ (5cm)

Diagram 5

Repeat, making a header and rod pocket at the lower edge of the panel.

3 Hemming the ruffles

Cut each 5″ (12.5cm) ruffle section in half crosswise into two 22½″ (57cm) sections. Stitch the ruffle sections together to make two 5″ (12.5cm) × approximately 153″ (389cm) ruffle strips. Use one 22½″ (57cm) long ruffle section and three 45″ (115cm) long ruffle sections for each strip.

Press under ½″ (1.3cm) on one long edge of one strip. Press under ½″ (1.3cm) again. Stitch close to the first fold, as shown in **Diagram 6.** Repeat, hemming all four edges of both ruffles.

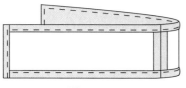

Diagram 6

4 Attaching the ruffles

Referring to **Diagram 7,** machine baste along one long edge of each ruffle, using two rows of stitches. Place the rows 1″ (2.5cm) and ½″ (1.3cm) from the edge. Divide and mark the edge into eight equal parts.

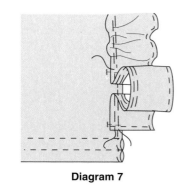

Diagram 7

🧵 SEW SIMPLE

When choosing thread, pick a color that is a shade darker than the fabric. Thread usually looks lighter when sewn.

Divide and mark the side edges of the panel, between the rod pockets, into eight equal parts.

Working on the right side of the panel, lap the ruffles over the long side edges between the rod pockets. Center the machine basting over the hem allowance. Match and pin at the markings.

Draw up the basting stitches, gathering the ruffle until it fits. Adjust the gathers; then topstitch the ruffle in place between the two rows of basting stitches, as shown in **Diagram 8.** Remove the basting stitches.

Diagram 8

5 **Making the tieback**

Stitch the two tieback sections together, as shown in **Diagram 9,** to make one 10″ × 90″ (25.5cm × 229cm) tieback.

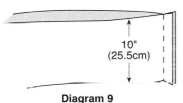

10″
(25.5cm)

Diagram 9

Fold the tieback in half lengthwise, with right sides together. Stitch ½″ (1.3cm) from the raw edges, leaving an opening for turning, as shown in **Diagram 10.** Turn the tieback right side out. Press. Slip stitch the opening closed, following the directions on page 126 for slip stitching.

Diagram 10

INSTALLATION

Hang the panel on the rods on the door. Wrap the tieback around the center, as shown in the photograph on page 112, and tie it in a bow, following the directions on page 128 for tying a bow.

✦ DESIGN PLUS

To make romantic panels for any standard window up to 36″ (91.5cm) wide, adjust the cutting length of the panel, as described in "Cutting Directions" on page 113. For each side of the panel, cut enough ruffle sections to equal two to two and a half times the measurement between the rods. Determine the tieback length after the panel is installed by wrapping a tape measure around the center and tying it in a bow.

Transform everyday curtains and drapes into spectacular window treatments with (clockwise, from upper left) Shirred, Pleated, Heart, or Quilted Tiebacks.

SHIRRED TIEBACKS

SUPPLIES

- *1¼ yards (1.2m) of 45" (115cm) wide decorator fabric, such as chintz, moiré, broadcloth, linen, or cotton blends*
- *½ yard (0.5m) of 45" (115cm) wide lining fabric, such as satin or silk-like polyester*
- *4 yards (3.7m) of 1" (2.5cm) diameter cotton cord*
- *Four 1" (2.5cm) plastic rings*
- *2 cup hooks*
- *1 large safety pin*
- *Fabric glue*

CUTTING DIRECTIONS

From the decorator fabric, cut one 3¼" (8.3cm) wide × approximately 420" (1,068cm) long continuous bias strip. Follow the directions on page 127 for making continuous bias strips. Cut the strip in half crosswise to make two approximately 210" (534cm) long strips.

From the lining fabric, cut four 3½" (9cm) wide × 45" (115cm) long strips.

Cut the cotton cord into two 70" (178cm) long pieces.

🧵 SEW SIMPLE

To keep the casing from slipping off the cord during the gathering process, secure the cord and the casing together at one end with a rubber band.

SEWING DIRECTIONS

Follow these directions for each tieback.

1 Covering the cord with lining

Lap and glue two strips of lining fabric together at the short ends, as shown in **Diagram 1.**

Diagram 1

Referring to **Diagram 2,** center the cotton cord on the strip. Fold one long edge of the strip under ½" (1.3cm). Lap and glue the folded edge over the other long edge, covering the cord. Let the glue dry. Trim the excess fabric at the ends of the cord.

Diagram 2

2 Making the shirred casing

With right sides together, fold one bias strip in half lengthwise. Stitch ½" (1.3cm) from the long cut edges, as shown in **Diagram 3.** Turn the casing right side out.

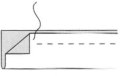

Diagram 3

Attach the safety pin to one end of the covered cotton cord. Feed the cord through the bias casing, as shown in **Diagram 4,** gathering the fabric evenly as you go.

Diagram 4

Referring to **Diagram 5,** turn in the ends of the casing. Slip stitch the opening closed, following the directions on page 126 for slip stitching. Catch the cording with the stitches.

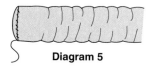

Diagram 5

3 **Finishing the tieback**

Tie a half-knot in one end of the cord, concealing the end in the center of the knot. Hand sew a plastic ring to the back of the knot, as shown in **Diagram 6.**

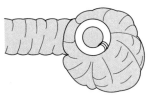

Diagram 6

Fold the tieback in half to find the center. Hand sew a plastic ring at the center back, as shown in **Diagram 7.**

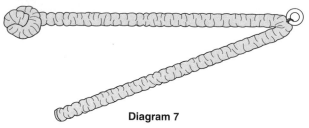

Diagram 7

Hand sew the unknotted end of the cord to the back of the knot, as shown in **Diagram 8.**

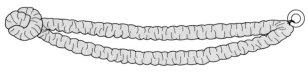

Diagram 8

INSTALLATION

Install the cup hooks at the desired height on the wall or window molding. Wrap the tiebacks around the drapery or curtain panels so the knot is on the outside, as shown in the photograph (upper left) on page 116, and hook the rings over the cup hooks.

⊕ DESIGN PLUS

For heavier curtains and drapes, use two cup hooks for each tieback. Install them 2" (5cm) apart on the molding. If the curtains or drapes extend beyond the window, install one hook on the wall and the other on the molding.

PLEATED TIEBACKS

SUPPLIES

- *1 yard (1m) of 54" (138cm) wide decorator fabric, such as chintz, moiré, broadcloth, linen, or cotton blends*

- *Four 1" (2.5cm) plastic rings*

- *Two 2½" (6.3cm) covered button forms*

- *One 8" × 16" (20.5cm × 40.5cm) piece of cardboard*

- *2 cup hooks*

- *Craft knife*

- *Fabric pleater, such as Clotilde's Perfect Pleater**

- *Hot-glue gun and glue sticks*

*If the Perfect Pleater is not available at local fabric or craft stores, it can be ordered through Clotilde Inc., 2 Sew Smart Way B8031, Stevens Point, WI 54481-8031; 800-772-2891.

CUTTING DIRECTIONS

From the decorator fabric, cut the following pieces, folding the fabric and using the patterns shown in **Diagram 1**:

- *Two 6" × 49½" (15cm × 126cm) tiebacks (A)*
- *Two 5" × 36½" (12.5cm × 92.5cm) rosettes (B)*
- *Two 6" (15cm) diameter rosette backs (C)*

From the remaining decorator fabric, cut the following:

- *Two 6" (15cm) square button covers*
- *Two 2" (5cm) wide × 20" (51cm) long bias strips*

From the cardboard, use the craft knife to cut two 5" (12.5cm) diameter circles.

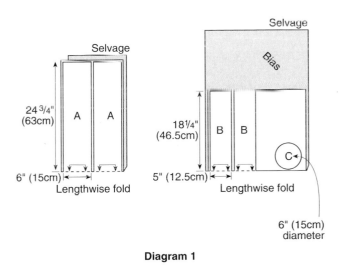

Diagram 1

SEWING DIRECTIONS

Follow these directions for each tieback.

1 Pleating the tieback

With right sides together, fold the tieback (A) in half lengthwise. Stitch ¼" (6mm) from each side edge, as shown in **Diagram 2**. Trim the corners.

Turn the tieback right side out. Press. Baste the raw edges together, as shown in **Diagram 3**.

Diagram 2   **Diagram 3**

🧵 SEW SIMPLE

When pleating, position the tieback so that the raw edges extend ½" (1.3cm) beyond the edge of the pleater. This extension makes it possible to machine stitch the pleats after pressing but before removing them from the pleater.

Press in ½" (1.3cm) deep pleats across the width of the tieback, following the pleater manufacturer's directions. To secure the pleats, machine stitch ⅜" (1cm) from the raw edge, as shown in **Diagram 4.**

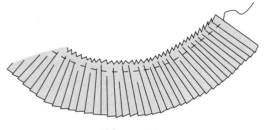

Diagram 4

Make double-fold bias tape from one of the bias strips, following the directions on page 127 for making bias tape. Stitch the bias tape to the raw edge of the tieback, as shown in **Diagram 5.** Hand sew one plastic ring to the bias tape at each end of the tieback.

Diagram 5

2 Making the rosette

Center and glue one cardboard circle to the wrong side of one rosette back (C). Fold the raw edges in over the cardboard and glue in place, as shown in **Diagram 6.**

Referring to **Diagram 7,** press under ¼" (6mm) on the short ends of one rosette (B). With the wrong sides together, fold the rosette in half lengthwise and press. Baste the raw edges together.

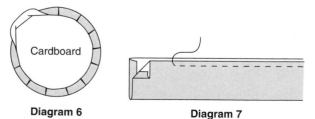

Cardboard

Diagram 6   Diagram 7

Press in ½" (1.3cm) deep pleats across the width of the rosette, following the pleater manufacturer's directions. To secure the pleats, machine stitch ⅜" (1cm) from the raw edge.

Arrange and glue the rosette in a circle to the cardboard side of the rosette back, as shown in **Diagram 8.** Lap and glue the ends together.

Cover the button form, following the manufacturer's directions. Glue the button to the center of the rosette, as shown in **Diagram 9.**

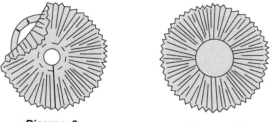

Diagram 8   Diagram 9

Place the rosette and tieback facedown, as shown in **Diagram 10,** and glue the front end of the tieback to the rosette back.

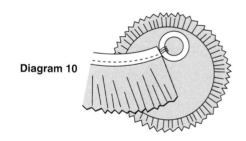

Diagram 10

INSTALLATION

Install the cup hooks at the desired height on the wall or the window molding. Wrap the tiebacks around the drapery or curtain panels, as shown in the photograph (upper right) on page 116, and hook the rings over the cup hooks.

⊕ DESIGN PLUS

To change the look of this tieback, use contrasting fabric for the bias binding and the covered button.

QUILTED TIEBACKS

SUPPLIES

- ⅜ yard (0.4m) of plaid fabric
- ½ yard (0.5m) of solid fabric
- ⅝ yard (0.6m) of printed fabric
- ⅜ yard (0.4m) of polyester batting
- 2 cup hooks
- Straight-edge ruler
- Water-soluble marking pen

CUTTING DIRECTIONS

All measurements include ¼" (6mm) seam allowances.

Use the straight-edge ruler and the water-soluble marking pen to measure and mark all of the shapes.

From the plaid fabric, cut:

- Twelve 2½" (6.3cm) squares (A)
- 3⅝ yards (3.4m) of 2" (5cm) wide bias strips. Follow the directions on page 127 for making bias strips.

From the solid fabric, cut:

- Four 1½" × 18" (3.8cm × 45.5cm) strips. Cut each strip into 1½" (3.8cm) squares, making 48 squares (B).
- Five 1⅞" × 18¾" (4.8cm × 47.5cm) strips. Cut each strip into 1⅞" (4.8cm) squares, making 48 squares. Cut each of these squares in half diagonally, making 96 triangles (C).

From the printed fabric, cut:

- Two 6" × 26" (15cm × 66cm) rectangles for the facing for the tieback.
- Five 1⅞" × 18¾" (4.8cm × 47.5cm) strips. Cut each strip into 1⅞" (4.8cm) squares, making 48 squares. Cut each of these squares in half diagonally, making 96 triangles (D).

From the batting, cut two 6" × 26" (15cm × 66cm) rectangles.

SEWING DIRECTIONS

1 Assembling the patchwork

Referring to **Diagram 1,** place one triangle C and one triangle D with right sides together and stitch along the diagonal edge. Press the seam open. Repeat, making 95 more pieced squares.

Referring to **Diagram 2,** stitch two of these squares together to form a rectangle. Press the seam open. Repeat, making 47 more small pieced rectangles.

Referring to **Diagram 3,** stitch one small pieced rectangle to the upper and lower edges of a large square A. Repeat, making 11 more large rectangles. Press the seams open.

Referring to **Diagram 4,** stitch a small square B to each short edge of the remaining small rectangles, making 24 narrow rectangles. Press the seams open.

Diagram 1

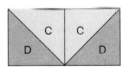

Diagram 2

Note: Diagrams do not reflect seam allowances on pieced triangles and squares.

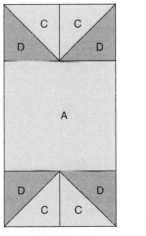

Diagram 3

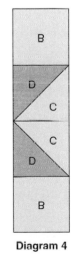

Diagram 4

Referring to **Diagram 5,** stitch a narrow rectangle to each side edge of a large rectangle. Repeat, making 11 more quilt blocks. Press the seams open.

Referring to **Diagram 6,** stitch six quilt blocks together to make one tieback front. Press the seams open. Repeat to make the other tieback front.

2 Quilting the tiebacks

Working on a large, flat surface, place the facing for one tieback wrong side up. Place the batting on top of the facing. Center one tieback front, right side up, over the batting. Hand baste the layers together, as shown in **Diagram 7,** ⅛" (3mm) from the edge of the tieback.

Machine stitch along each seam, except where the triangle Cs are joined, as shown in **Diagram 8.**

Repeat for the other tieback.

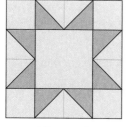

Diagram 5

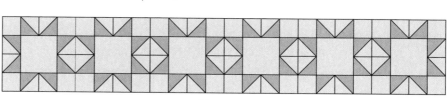

Diagram 6

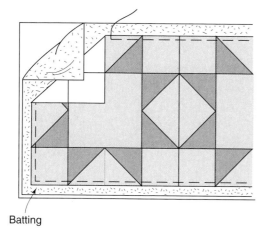

Batting

Diagram 7

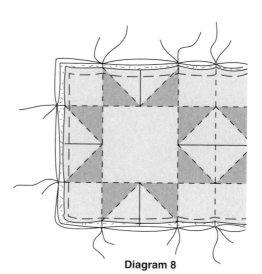

Diagram 8

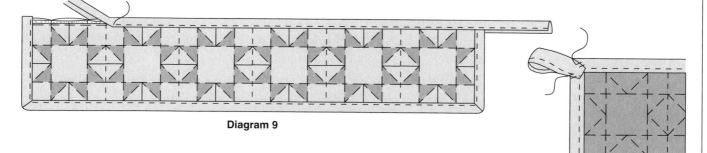

Diagram 9

Diagram 10

3 Finishing the tiebacks

Make double-fold bias tape from the bias strips, following the directions on page 127 for making bias tape. Referring to **Diagram 9,** apply the tape to the side and lower edges of one tieback, following the directions on page 127 for applying bias tape and just covering the machine basting stitches. Apply the binding to the upper edge, extending each end of the tape 2½" (6.3cm) beyond the sides of the tieback.

Fold each end of the bias tape to the facing side of the tieback and hand sew in place, as shown in **Diagram 10.**

Repeat for the other tieback.

HEART TIEBACKS

SUPPLIES

- ¼ yard (0.3m) each of five different color fabrics
- 3⅝ yards (3.4m) each of five different color ⅜" (9mm) wide picot-edge satin ribbon
- 5 ounces (140 grams) of polyester fiberfill
- Tracing paper
- Liquid ravel preventer, such as Fray Check
- 2 cup hooks

CUTTING DIRECTIONS

Trace the hearts, as shown in **Diagram 1** on page 124, to create the patterns for hearts A, B, C, D, and E.

From fabric 1, cut four heart As.

From fabric 2, cut eight heart Bs.

From fabric 3, cut eight heart Cs.

From fabric 4, cut eight heart Ds.

From fabric 5, cut eight heart Es.

From the ribbon, cut four 32" (81.5cm) long pieces of each color.

INSTALLATION

Install the cup hooks at the desired height on the wall or window molding. Wrap the tiebacks around the drapery or curtain panels, as shown in the photograph (lower left) on page 116. Hook the loops onto the cup hooks.

⊕ **DESIGN PLUS**

For a bolder look, replace the cup hooks with push pin holdbacks—decorative hardware that is meant to show!

SEWING DIRECTIONS

Follow these directions for each tieback.

1 Making the hearts

With right sides together, stitch two heart As together ¼" (6mm) from the cut edge; leave an opening along one side edge large enough for turning and stuffing. Trim the corners and clip the curves, as shown in **Diagram 2.** Repeat, using four each of hearts B, C, and D.

Diagram 2

With right sides together, stitch two heart Es together ¼" (6mm) from the cut edge. Leave an opening between the two dots, as shown in **Diagram 3,** for turning, stuffing, and inserting the ribbons. Trim the corners and clip the curves. Repeat, stitching two more heart Es together.

Diagram 3

Turn all nine hearts right side out. Stuff with polyester fiberfill. Slip stitch the openings closed on hearts A, B, C, and D, following the directions on page 126 for slip stitching.

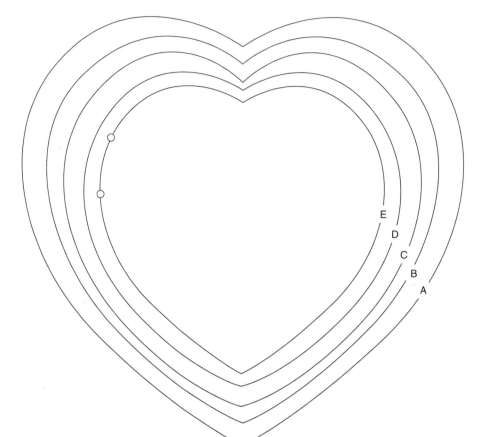

Diagram 1

2 Finishing the tieback

Arrange the hearts in size order, as shown in **Diagram 4.** Hand sew the hearts together.

Referring to **Diagram 5,** lay one of each color ribbon together and pin at one end. Insert the ribbons into one of the ribbon openings. Slip stitch the opening closed, as shown in **Diagram 6.** Follow the directions on page 126 for slip stitching.

Finish the other end of the tieback in the same manner. Seal the ends of the ribbons with liquid ravel preventer.

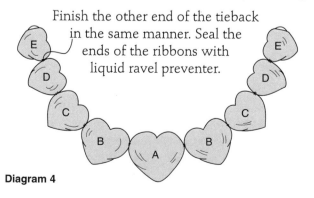

Diagram 4

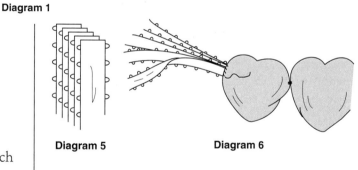

Diagram 5   **Diagram 6**

INSTALLATION

Install the cup hooks at the desired height on the wall or the window molding. Wrap the tiebacks around the drapery or curtain panels, as shown in the photograph (lower right) on page 116. Tie the ribbons in a bow. Hook the ribbons over the cup hook.

🧵 SEW SIMPLE

A chopstick makes a good stuffing tool.

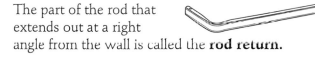
This section is a compilation of tips, techniques, and general information that will make it easier to complete the projects in this book.

HARDWARE

These are the hardware and accessory terms you'll find used throughout this book.

CURTAIN RODS

Café curtain rod: A decorative curtain rod.

Continental rod: A wide, flat version of the standard curtain rod.

Decorative pole rod and rings: A thick, round, ornamental rod made of wood, metal, or plastic with coordinating rings. The drapes are usually attached to the bottom of the rings with pleater hooks.

Double curtain rod: Two standard curtain rods installed on a set of double brackets.

Sash rod: A flat or round rod with shallow mounting brackets. It is used to install a lightweight window treatment close to the glass.

Spring tension rod: A round rod that expands to fit inside the window frame. It does not require brackets or mounting screws.

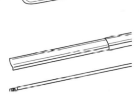

Standard curtain rod: A flat, narrow, utilitarian rod that is mounted on the wall or window frame.

The part of the rod that extends out at a right angle from the wall is called the **rod return.**

ACCESSORIES AND SPECIAL EFFECTS

Angle iron: An L-shaped bracket, most commonly used to install a mounting board at the window.

Butterfly Ladder: The brand name for a lightweight plastic grid that can be mounted across the top of a window. Fabric is pulled through the grid openings, creating interesting decorative effects.

Curtain hooks: Small pin-on hooks used to attach a window treatment without a rod pocket to a standard curtain rod.

Drapery hooks: 3" (7.5cm) long, pan-shaped hooks with mounting screws.

Locking pleater hooks: Extra-long pleater hooks for hanging pleated drapes from decorative rings.

Mounting board: A precut 1" × 2" (2.5cm × 5cm) length of wood. Soft fabric shades are stapled to a mounting board; then, with the aid of angle irons or screws, the board is secured at the top of the window.

Nylon cable cord: Narrow, braided cord, generally $\frac{1}{16}$" or $\frac{1}{8}$" (1.5mm or 3mm) in diameter.

Pleater tape: A woven tape with vertical pockets. Soft pinch pleats are formed by inserting four-pronged pleater hooks in the pockets.

Push pin holdbacks: Push pins with large, decorative heads, which are used to permanently secure a window treatment.

Ring tape: Twill tape with plastic rings attached every 5″ or 6″ (12.5cm or 15cm).

Screw eyes: Metal rings that are screwed into a furring strip or a mounting board.

Shirring tape: A woven tape with two or four draw cords. Gathers form when the cords are pulled up.

Tieback bracket: Any non-decorative plastic or metal drapery holdback that is attached directly to a window frame or wall.

Tieback wedge: A V-shaped tieback bracket with a pointed end that is pushed into a window frame or wall.

Tulip-shaped swag holder: A U-shaped holder on a bracket base.

Weight rod: A long metal rod, approximately ½″ (1.3cm) in diameter, which is attached across the bottom of certain styles of soft fabric shades to add weight and stability.

Weighted shade pull: A metal sinker that is attached to the end of a pull cord.

Window cleat: A metal cleat used to anchor the excess pull cord when a soft fabric shade is raised.

STITCHING TERMS

These are the stitching terms you'll find used throughout this book.

SLIP STITCHING

Slip stitching provides a neat, almost invisible way to secure two turned-under edges together by hand.

To begin, knot the end of the thread. Bury the knot in the fold of the fabric. Working from right to left and referring to **Diagram 1,** pick up a single fabric thread just below the folded edge. Insert the needle into the fold directly above the first stitch and bring it out ¼″ (6mm) away. Pick up another single thread in the project directly below the point where the needle just emerged.

Diagram 1

UNDERSTITCHING

Understitching is a row of machine stitching that keeps the lining from rolling to the outside of the project.

After stitching the seam, press the seam allowances toward the lining. Working from the right side, stitch ⅛″ (3mm) from the seam line, through the lining and seam allowances only, as shown in **Diagram 2.**

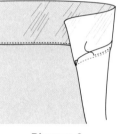

Diagram 2

NO-SEW HEMMING

On the wrong side of the fabric, apply a strip of paper-backed fusible web, such as Pellon Wonder-Under, ⅜″ (1cm) from the raw edge, as shown in **Diagram 3.** Press the fabric up along the outer edge of the paper. Fold the fabric up so that the first fold just covers the paper. Press, creasing the paper. Open out the folds. Peel off the paper. Refold the fabric and press lightly. Fuse, following the manufacturer's directions.

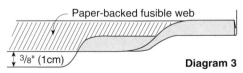

Paper-backed fusible web

⅜″ (1cm)

Diagram 3

To eliminate bulk at a point, first fuse the upper and lower edges of the panel. Apply the paper-backed fusible web to the side edges as directed above. Before removing the paper, open out the first fold.

Trim the extending side hem allowance to match the intersecting upper or lower edge of the panel, as shown in **Diagram 4**. Peel off the paper, refold the fabric, press lightly, and fuse, following the manufacturer's directions.

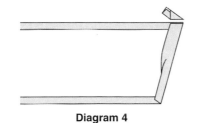

Diagram 4

BIAS TAPE

MAKING CONTINUOUS BIAS STRIPS

Cut a rectangle of fabric. Trim each side of the rectangle to exactly follow a thread of the fabric. Fold down one corner of the rectangle until the lengthwise and crosswise edges meet, as shown in **Diagram 5**. Press along the fold; open out the fabric.

Cut a cardboard strip equal to the width of bias needed for your project. Using this cardboard as a template and beginning at the fold, mark parallel lines with a pencil on the wrong side of the fabric, as shown in **Diagram 6**. Stop marking when you reach a corner. Cut off the two triangles of unmarked fabric, as shown in **Diagram 7**.

Referring to **Diagram 8,** fold the fabric, with right sides together, into a tube. Match the pencil lines so that one width of binding extends beyond the edge on each side. Sew a ¼" (6mm) seam. Press the seam open. Starting at one end, cut along the marked line, continuing around the tube until there is one continuous strip.

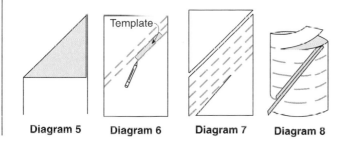

| **Diagram 5** | **Diagram 6** | **Diagram 7** | **Diagram 8** |

MAKING DOUBLE-FOLD BIAS TAPE

To make double-fold bias tape from a continuous bias strip, place the bias strip wrong side up on an ironing board. Referring to **Diagram 9**, fold one long edge under an amount equal to one-quarter of the original width of the strip; press. Fold the other long edge under so that the long raw edges almost meet at the center of the strip; press. Fold the bias lengthwise so that one long edge extends slightly below the other; press.

Diagram 9

APPLYING DOUBLE-FOLD BIAS TAPE

Encase the raw edge of the project in the bias tape, positioning the wider side of the tape on the wrong side of the project. Pin, securing all of the layers. On the right side of the project, stitch along the edge of the tape through all of the layers, as shown in **Diagram 10**.

To apply the tape at a corner, encase one edge all the way to the intersecting raw edge of the project, as shown in **Diagram 11**. Fold the tape down, encasing the intersecting raw edge, and pin in place, as shown in **Diagram 12**. Finger press the excess tape at the corner on both sides of the project into diagonal folds. On the right side, insert the machine needle into the tape at the edge of the fold. Stitch along the edge through all of the layers.

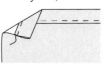

Diagram 10

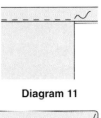

Diagram 11

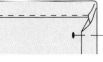

Diagram 12

STENCILING

PREPARING A STENCIL

Place the printed design over your stencil acetate with a piece of graphite paper in between. Trace the design with a pencil.

Use a craft knife to cut out the design, carefully following the traced lines. To help keep a sharp edge and prevent the stencil from tearing, change the knife blade often.

It may be necessary to reverse the design to get a mirror image. To do this, either make a second stencil, reversing the direction of the design, or turn the same stencil over and use the other side. For the latter, stencil the first side of the design. Wipe off the excess paint. Spray with a fixative, such as Krylon, to seal the paint, following the manufacturer's directions. Let the stencil dry for at least 15 minutes; then turn it over and stencil the design in reverse.

PLANNING A STENCIL DESIGN

To figure out how to work a design around a curve or corner, cut out the curtain or valance shape from white craft paper. Play with the design, tracing it onto the paper. To achieve the desired effect around a corner or curve, it may be necessary to leave out part of a design.

Some designs work better if you start stenciling at the center and work out to the edges.

APPLYING STENCIL PAINT

Hold the stencil brush straight up. Use a dabbing or circular motion to get the paint out of the container and onto the brush.

Position the stencil on the fabric. Using the same circular motion with the brush, apply the paint to the stencil, as shown in **Diagram 13.** Because it takes very little paint to fill in the stencil, it is better to apply a few light layers of paint rather than one heavy one.

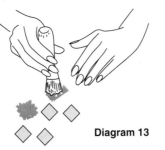

Diagram 13

Test the stencil on a scrap of the actual fabric before stenciling your window treatment. If not enough paint is getting through, slightly enlarge the stencil opening. Be careful. Enlarging it too much may weaken the stencil.

A torn stencil can be temporarily patched with Scotch Magic tape. Place a piece of tape over the tear on both sides of the stencil. If the tape overlaps into the stencil openings, use the craft knife to recut the design.

To apply more than one color of paint to a design, use Scotch Magic tape to cover the stencil openings that are not for the paint color you are using.

Oiled stencil paper can be used in place of stencil acetate. However, it requires some additional handling techniques.

- Trace the design onto the rough side of the paper.
- If the stencil will be used several times, varnish or shellac the paper after the design has been cut out. This will help make the stencil sturdier.
- Position the stencil rough side down on the fabric.

TYING A BOW

Referring to **Diagrams 14** and **15,** fold the ribbon or bow section in half lengthwise. Tie a half-knot at the center.

Fold the bottom end to one side and back over on itself, forming a loop, as shown in **Diagram 16.**

Bring the other end over the loop, then under and up between the loop and the half-knot, as shown in **Diagram 17,** to form the knot and the second loop at the same time.

Pull both loops tight until they are an even size and the ends an even length, as shown in **Diagram 18.**

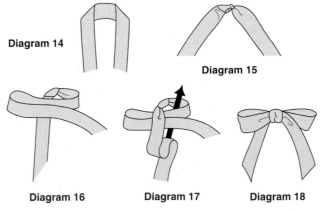

Diagram 14

Diagram 15

Diagram 16   Diagram 17   Diagram 18